FIRST 50 SONGS

YOU SHOULD PLAY ON HARMONICA

Arranged by Tad Dreis

ISBN 978-1-4950-5022-0

HAL•LEONARD®
CORPORATION
7777 W. BLUEMOUND RD. P.O. BOX 13819 MILWAUKEE, WI 53213

Visit Hal Leonard Online at
www.halleonard.com

Ain't No Sunshine

Words and Music by Bill Withers

C diatonic harmonica

*Harmonica sounds one octave higher than written.

Bridge

N.C.

I	know,	I	know,	I	know,	I	know,	I	know,	I
7↑	8↓	7↑	8↓	7↑	8↓	7↑	8↓	6↓	7↑	8↓	7↑

know,	I	know,	I	know,	I	know,	I	know,	I	know,
8↓	7↑	8↓	7↑	8↓	6↓	7↑	8↓	7↑	9↓	8↓	8↓

	I	know,	I	know,	I	know,	I	know,	I	know,
	7↑	8↓	7↑	8↓	7↑	8↓	7↑	8↓	7↑	8↓

I	know,	I	know,	I	know,	I	know,	I	know,	I
7↑	8↓	7↑	8↓	7↑	8↓	7↑	8↓	7↑	8↓	8↓

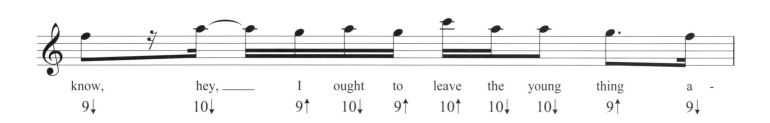

know,	hey,	I	ought	to	leave	the	young	thing	a -
9↓	10↓	9↑	10↓	9↑	10↑	10↓	10↓	9↑	9↓

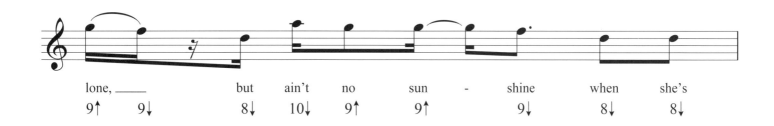

lone,		but	ain't	no	sun -	shine	when	she's
9↑	9↓	8↓	10↓	9↑	9↑	9↓	8↓	8↓

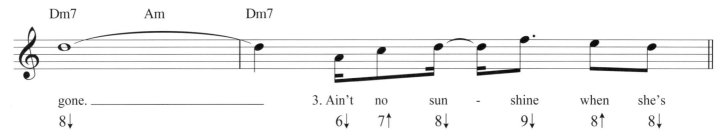

gone. _____ 3. Ain't no sun - shine when she's

8↓   6↓   7↑   8↓   9↓   8↑   8↓

Coda

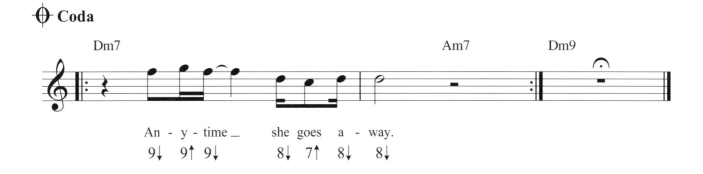

An - y - time ___ she goes a - way.

9↓   9↑   9↓   8↓   7↑   8↓   8↓

Additional Lyrics

2. Wonder this time where she's gone,
Wonder if she's gone to stay.
Ain't no sunshine when she's gone.
And this house just ain't no home
Anytime she goes away.

3. Ain't no sunshine when she's gone,
Only darkness every day.
Ain't no sunshine when she's gone,
And this house just ain't no home
Anytime she goes away.

Amazing Grace

Words by John Newton
From A Collection of Sacred Ballads
Traditional American Melody
From Carrell and Clayton's Virginia Harmony
Arranged by Edwin O. Excell

C diatonic harmonica

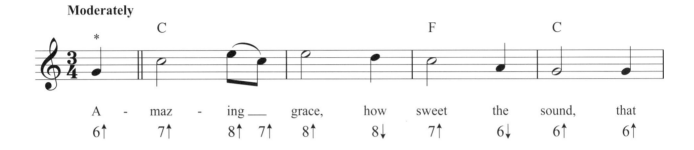

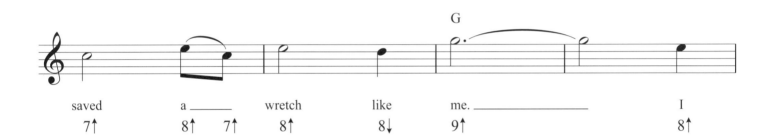

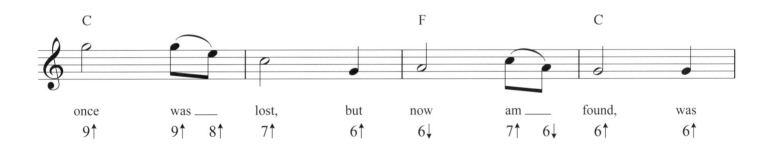

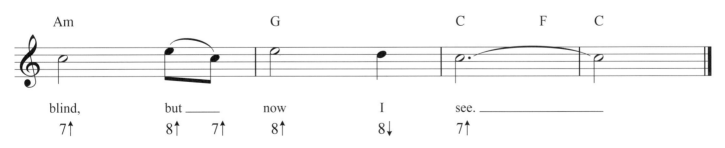

*Harmonica sounds one octave higher than written.

All My Loving

Words and Music by John Lennon and Paul McCartney

C diatonic harmonica

Chorus

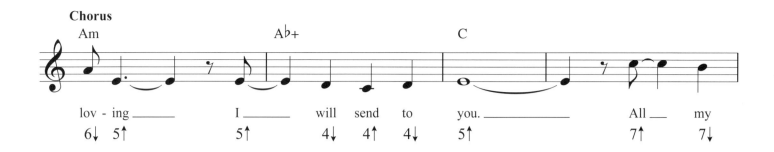

lov - ing _____ I _____ will send to you. _____ All _____ my
6↓ 5↑   5↑   4↓ 4↑ 4↓   5↑   7↑   7↓

To Coda ⊕

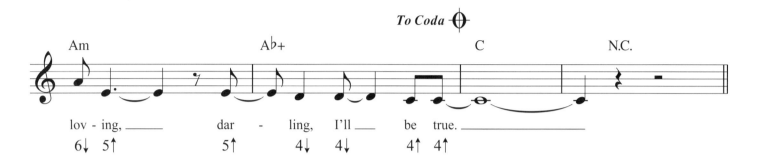

lov - ing, _____ dar - ling, I'll _____ be true. _____
6↓ 5↑   5↑   4↓ 4↓   4↑ 4↑

Interlude

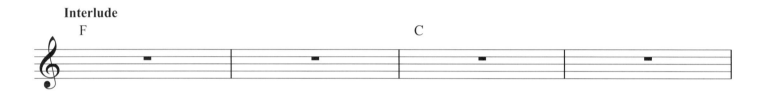

D.S. al Coda
(take 2nd ending)

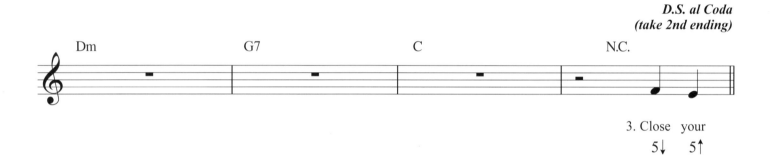

3. Close your
5↓ 5↑

⊕ **Coda**

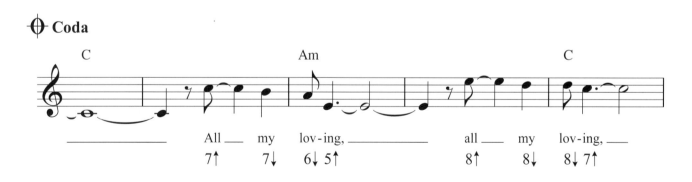

_____ All _____ my lov-ing, _____ all _____ my lov-ing, _____
7↑   7↓ 6↓ 5↑   8↑   8↓ 8↓ 7↑

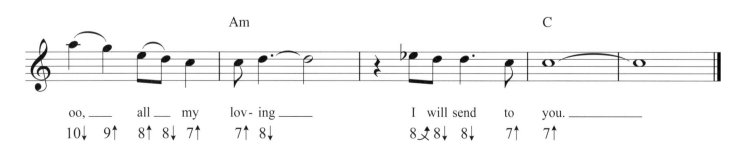

oo, _____ all _____ my lov- ing _____ I will send to you. _____
10↓ 9↑ 8↑ 8↓ 7↑   7↑ 8↓   8↗ 8↓ 8↓   7↑ 7↑

Blowin' in the Wind

Words and Music by Bob Dylan

C diatonic harmonica

*Harmonica sounds one octave higher than written.

The Boxer

Words and Music by Paul Simon

C diatonic harmonica

Verse
Moderately fast

1. I am just a poor boy. Though my sto - ry's sel - dom told, I have
6↑ 6↑ 6↑ 6↓ 6↑ 5↑ 5↑ 5↓ 6↑ 6↑ 7↑ 7↓ 6↓ 6↓ 7↓

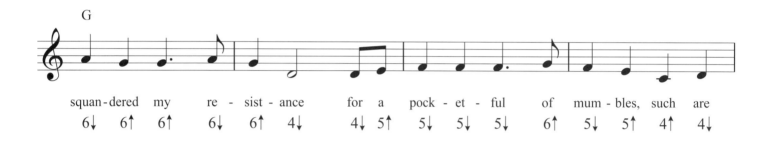

squan - dered my re - sist - ance for a pock - et - ful of mum - bles, such are
6↓ 6↑ 6↑ 6↓ 6↑ 4↓ 4↓ 5↑ 5↓ 5↓ 5↓ 6↑ 5↓ 5↑ 4↑ 4↓

prom - is - es. _____ All lies and jest, still a man hears what he
5↓ 5↑ 4↑ 7↑ 7↑ 7↓ 7↑ 7↑ 7↑ 7↑ 7↓ 7↓ 7↓

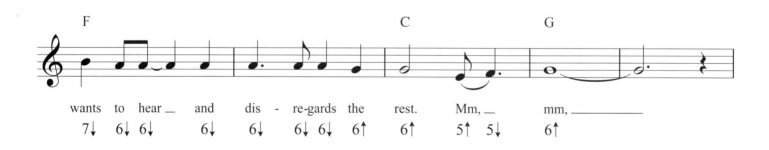

wants to hear __ and dis - re-gards the rest. Mm, __ mm, _____
7↓ 6↓ 6↓ 6↓ 6↓ 6↓ 6↓ 6↑ 6↑ 5↑ 5↓ 6↑

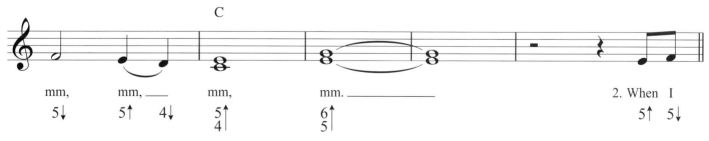

mm, mm, ____ mm, mm. _____ 2. When I
5↓ 5↑ 4↓ 5↑/4 6↑/5 5↑ 5↓

*Harmonica sounds one octave higher than written.

Verse

left my home and my fam - i - ly, ___ I was no more than a
6↑ 6↑ 6↑ 6↑ 6↑ 6↑ 5↓ 5↑ 5↑ 5↓ 6↑ 7↑ 7↑ 7↓

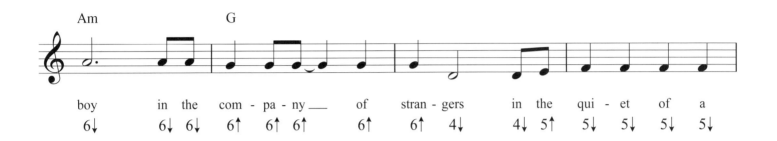

boy in the com - pa - ny ___ of stran - gers in the qui - et of a
6↓ 6↓ 6↓ 6↑ 6↑ 6↑ 6↑ 6↑ 4↓ 4↓ 5↑ 5↓ 5↓ 5↓ 5↓

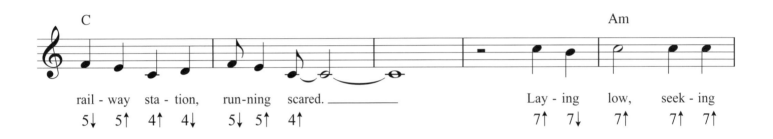

rail - way sta - tion, run - ning scared. _____ Lay - ing low, seek - ing
5↓ 5↑ 4↑ 4↓ 5↓ 5↑ 4↑ 7↑ 7↓ 7↑ 7↑ 7↑

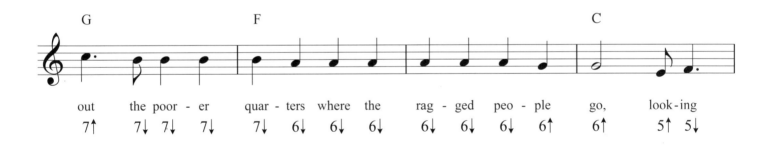

out the poor - er quar - ters where the rag - ged peo - ple go, look - ing
7↑ 7↓ 7↓ 7↓ 7↓ 6↓ 6↓ 6↓ 6↓ 6↓ 6↓ 6↑ 6↑ 5↑ 5↓

for the plac - es on - ly they would know. Lie, la,
6↑ 4↓ 4↓ 5↑ 5↓ 5↓ 5↑ 4↓ 4↑ 7↑ 7↓

Chorus

lie, lie, la, lie, la, lie, la, lie. Lie, la,
7↑ 7↑ 7↓ 7↑ 7↓ 7↓ 6↓ 6↑ 7↑ 7↓

10

lie,　　　　　　　lie, la, lie, la, lie, la, lie,＿＿ la, la, la, la,
7↑　　　　　　　8↓ 8↑ 9↓ 8↑ 8↓ 7↑ 8↓　　7↑ 7↑ 7↑ 7↓

lie.＿＿＿＿＿　　　　　　　　　　　　　　3. Ask - ing
7↑　　　　　　　　　　　　　　　　　　5↑ 5↓

Verse

on - ly work-man's wag - es, I come look-ing for a job. But I get no of -
6↑ 6↑ 6↑ 6↑　6↑ 5↑ 5↑ 5↑　5↓ 5↑　4↑ 4↓　5↑　5↑ 5↑ 5↑ 5↑ 5↑

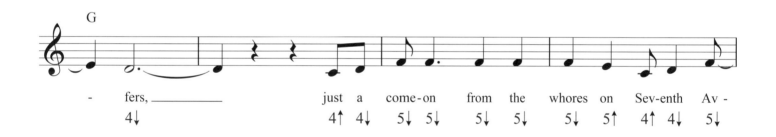

- fers,＿＿＿＿＿　　just a come-on from the whores on Sev-enth Av -
4↓　　　　　　4↑ 4↓　5↓ 5↓　5↓ 5↓　5↓ 5↑　4↑ 4↓ 5↓

- e - nue.＿＿＿＿　　　　I do de - clare,　there were times＿
5↑ 5↑　　　　　　　　7↑ 7↑ 7↓　7↑　　7↑ 7↑ 7↑

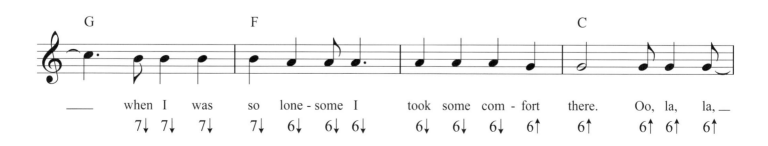

＿＿ when I was so lone - some I took some com - fort there. Oo, la, la,＿
7↓ 7↓ 7↓　7↓ 6↓ 6↓ 6↓　6↓ 6↓ 6↓ 6↑　6↑　6↑ 6↑ 6↑

la, la, la, la.
6↑ 6↑ 6↑ 6↑

4. Then I'm
5↑ 5↓

Verse

lay - ing out my win - ter clothes _ and wish - ing I was gone, _ go - ing
6↑ 6↑ 6↑ 6↑ 6↑ 5↓ 5↑ 5↓ 6↑ 7↑ 7↑ 7↓ 6↓ 6↓ 5↑

home where the New York Cit - y win - ters are - n't
6↑ 4↓ 5↑ 5↓ 5↓ 5↓ 5↓ 5↓ 5↑ 4↑ 4↓

bleed - ing me, _ lead - ing me, _
5↓ 5↑ 5↑ 7↑ 7↓ 6↑ 6↓

go - ing home. _
6↓ 5↑ 6↑

5. In the
6↑ 6↓

Verse

clear - ing stands a box - er, and a fight - er by his trade. And he
6↑ 6↑ 6↑ 6↑ 6↑ 5↑ 5↑ 5↓ 6↑ 6↑ 7↑ 7↓ 6↓ 6↓ 7↓

12

car - ries   the   re - mind - ers   of   ev -'ry   glove   that   laid him   down ___   or
6↓   6↑   6↑   6↓   6↑   4↓   4↓   5↓   5↓   5↓   5↓   5↓   5↑   4↑   4↓

cut   him   'til   he   cried ____   out   in his   an - ger   and his   shame, _   "I   am
5↓   5↑   4↑   4↓   5↓   5↑   6↑   6↑   6↑   7↑   7↑   7↓   7↑   7↑   7↑

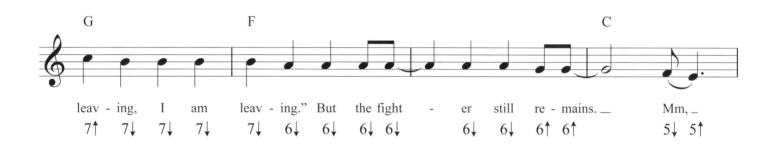

leav - ing,   I   am   leav - ing."   But   the fight   -   er   still   re - mains. __   Mm, _
7↑   7↓   7↓   7↓   7↓   6↓   6↓   6↓   6↓   6↓   6↓   6↑   6↑   5↓   5↑

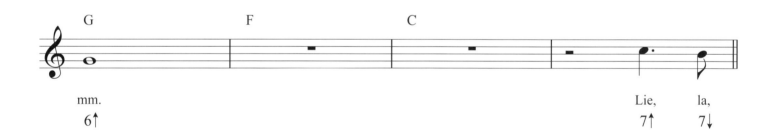

mm.   Lie,   la,
6↑   7↑   7↓

Outro-Chorus

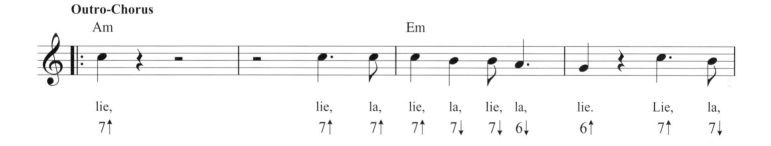

lie,   lie,   la,   lie,   la,   lie,   la,   lie.   Lie,   la,
7↑   7↑   7↑   7↑   7↓   7↓   6↓   6↑   7↑   7↓

Repeat and fade

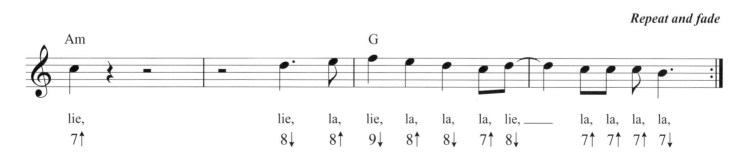

lie,   lie,   la,   lie,   la,   la,   la,   lie, _____   la,   la,   la,   la,
7↑   8↓   8↑   9↓   8↑   8↓   7↑   8↓   7↑   7↑   7↑   7↓

Brown Eyed Girl

Words and Music by Van Morrison

C diatonic harmonica

*Harmonica sounds one octave higher than written.

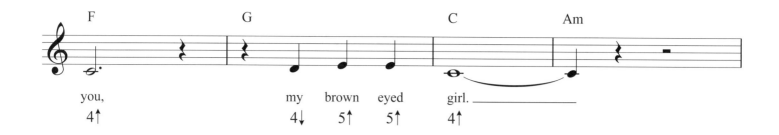

you,   my   brown   eyed   girl. _____

4↑   4↓   5↑   5↑   4↑

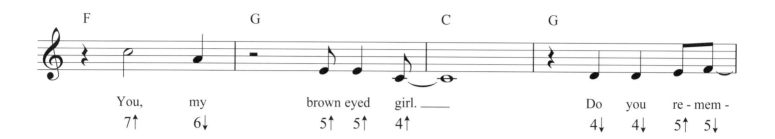

You,   my   brown eyed   girl. ____   Do   you   re - mem -

7↑   6↓   5↑   5↑   4↑   4↓   4↓   5↑   5↓

Chorus

- ber when   we   used   to   sing, ____ "Sha,   la, ____   la,   la, ___

5↓   6↑   5↓   5↑   4↓   4↑   6↑   6↑   6↑   6↓

___ la,   la, ____ la,   la, _____ la,   la,   la,   te,   da? ____

6↓   6↓   6↓   6↑   6↑   6↑   5↑   5↑   4↓

Sha,   la, ____ la,   la, _____ la,   la, ____ la,   la, _____ la,   la,   la,   te,   da, ___

6↑   6↑   6↑   6↓   6↓   6↓   6↓   6↑   6↑   6↑   5↑   5↑   4↓

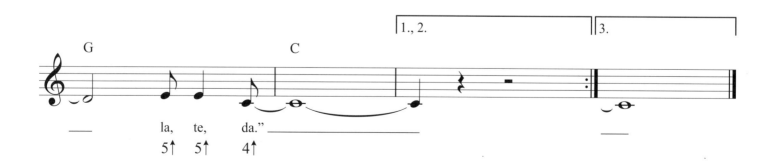

___   la,   te,   da." _____

5↑   5↑   4↑

Bye Bye Love

Words and Music by Felice Bryant and Boudleaux Bryant

C diatonic harmonica

Verse

Moderately fast

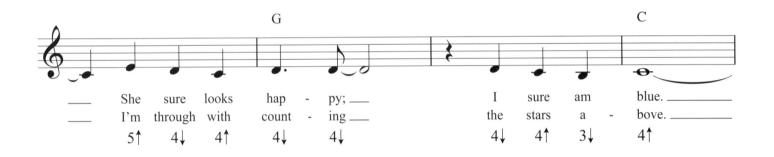

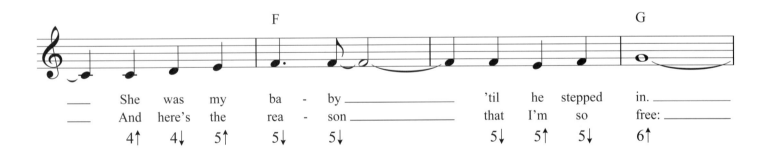

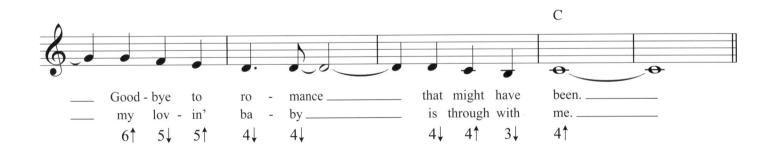

Chorus

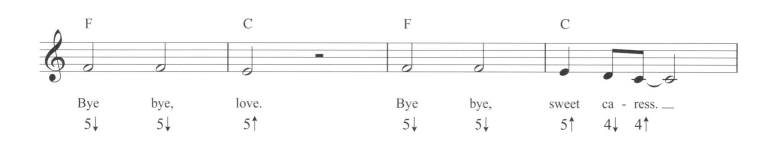

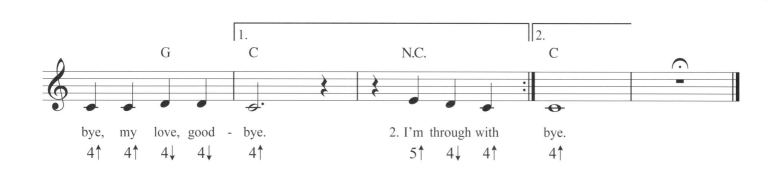

Easy

Words and Music by Walter Horton

C diatonic harmonica

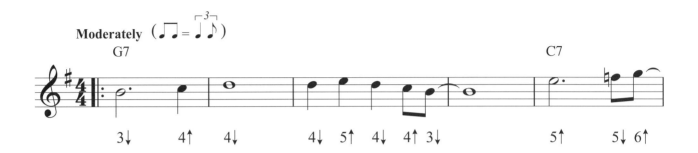

Edelweiss
from THE SOUND OF MUSIC
Lyrics by Oscar Hammerstein II
Music by Richard Rodgers

C diatonic harmonica

*Harmonica sounds one octave higher than written.

Goodnight, Irene

Words and Music by Huddie Ledbetter and John A. Lomax

C diatonic harmonica

*Harmonica sounds one octave higher than written.

I'm an Old Cowhand
(From the Rio Grande)

Words and Music by Johnny Mercer

C diatonic harmonica

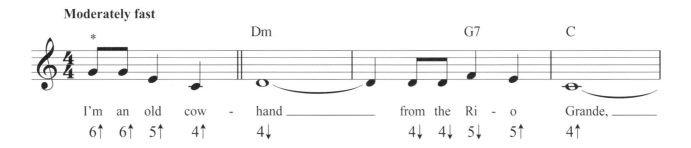

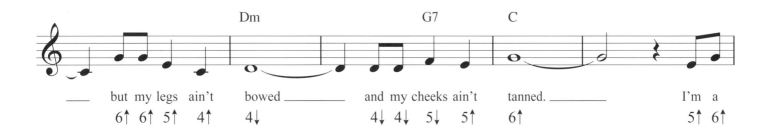

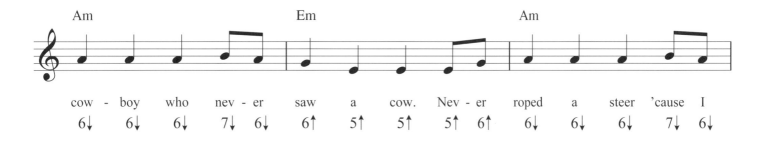

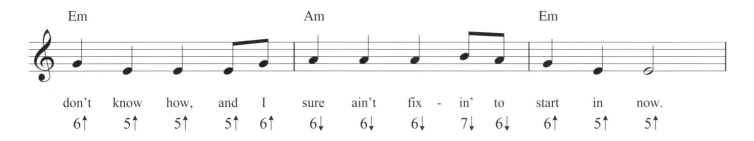

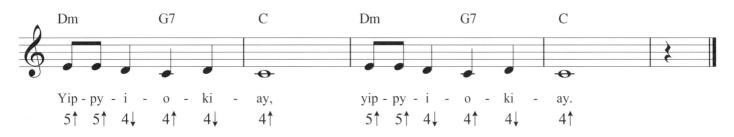

*Harmonica sounds one octave higher than written.

Happy Birthday to You

Words and Music by Mildred J. Hill and Patty S. Hill

C diatonic harmonica

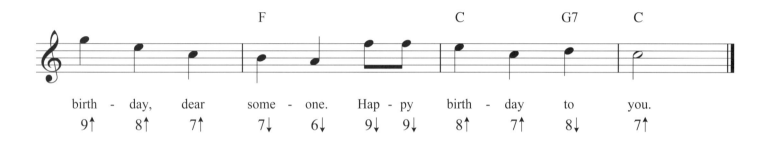

*Harmonica sounds one octave higher than written.

He's Got the Whole World in His Hands

Traditional Spiritual

C diatonic harmonica

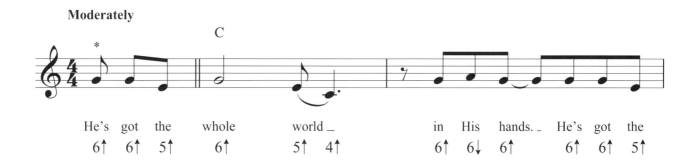

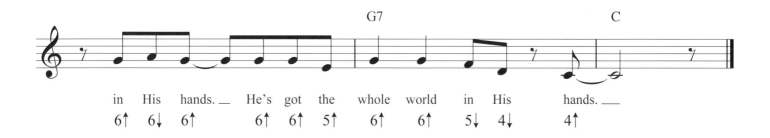

*Harmonica sounds one octave higher than written.

In the Good Old Summertime

Words by Ren Shields
Music by George Evans

C diatonic harmonica

*Harmonica sounds one octave higher than written.

Isn't She Lovely

Words and Music by Stevie Wonder

C diatonic harmonica

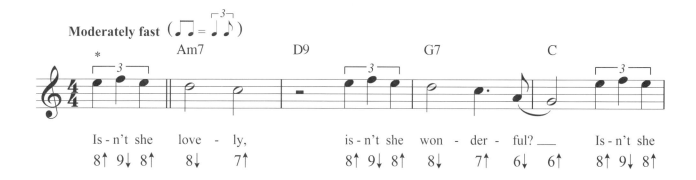

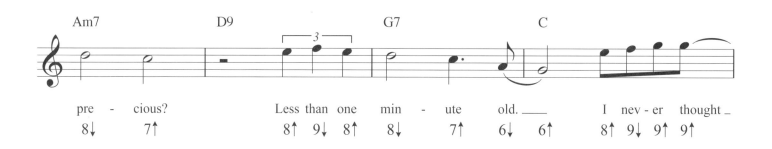

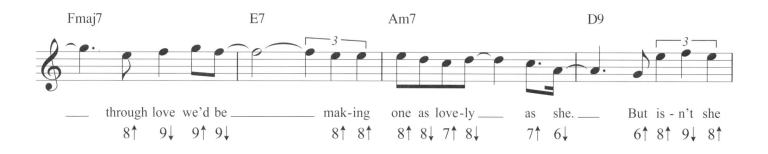

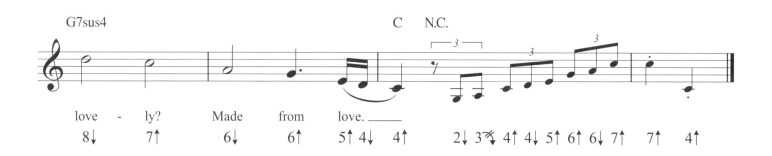

*Harmonica sounds one octave higher than written.

Jamaica Farewell

Words and Music by Irving Burgie

C diatonic harmonica

Verse
Moderately

C   F   G7

Down the way where the nights are gay __ and the sun shines dai - ly on the
6↑ 6↑ 6↑ 6↑ 6↑ 6↓ 7↓ 7↑ 7↓ 6↓ 6↑ 6↑ 5↓ 5↓ 5↓ 5↓

C   F

moun-tain top,   I took a trip on a sail - ing ship __ and when I
5↑ 5↓ 6↑   6↑ 6↑ 6↑ 6↑ 6↑ 6↑ 6↓ 7↓ 7↑ 7↑ 7↓ 6↓

Chorus

G7   C   C   Dm

reached Ja-mai - ca I made a stop. But I'm sad to say I'm on my way, __
6↑ 6↑ 5↓ 5↓ 5↓ 5↑ 4↓ 4↑ 5↑ 6↑ 4↑ 4↑ 5↑ 5↑ 4↓ 4↓ 5↓

G7   C

won't be back for man - y a day. My heart is down, __ my head is
3↓ 4↑ 4↓ 3↓ 4↑ 4↑ 4↑ 5↑ 6↑ 4↑ 4↑ 5↑ 5↑ 5↑ 5↑

Dm   G7   C

turn-ing a - round. __ I had to leave a lit - tle girl in King - ston town.
4↓ 4↓ 4↓ 5↓ 5↓ 5↓ 5↓ 5↑ 5↑ 5↑ 5↑ 4↓ 4↓ 4↓ 4↑ 4↑

*Harmonica sounds one octave higher than written.

Juke

Words and Music by Walter Jacobs

C diatonic harmonica

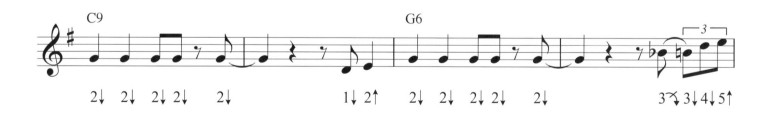

Jambalaya
(On the Bayou)

Words and Music by Hank Williams

C diatonic harmonica

Verse

Moderately

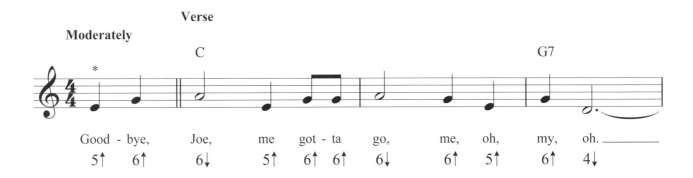

Good - bye, Joe, me got - ta go, me, oh, my, oh. ____

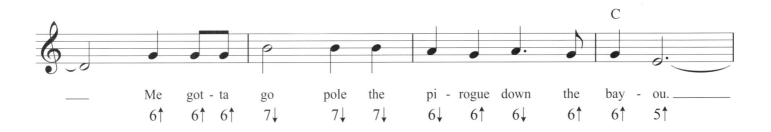

____ Me got - ta go pole the pi - rogue down the bay - ou. ____

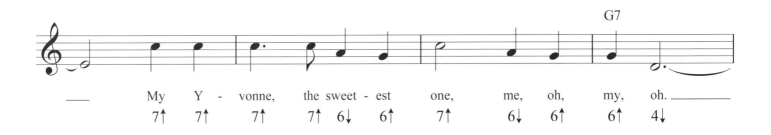

____ My Y - vonne, the sweet - est one, me, oh, my, oh. ____

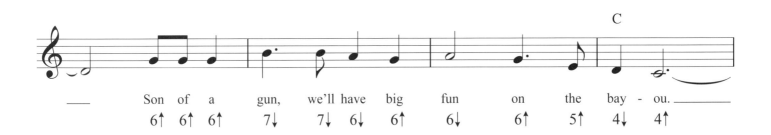

____ Son of a gun, we'll have big fun on the bay - ou. ____

*Harmonica sounds one octave higher than written.

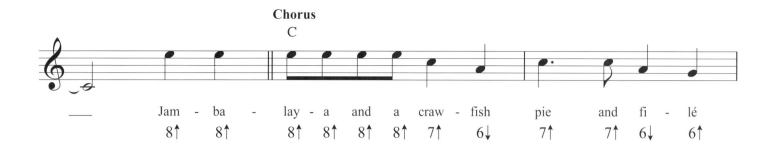

Jam - ba - lay - a and a craw - fish pie and fi - lé

8↑ 8↑ 8↑ 8↑ 8↑ 8↑ 7↑ 6↓ 7↑ 7↑ 6↓ 6↑

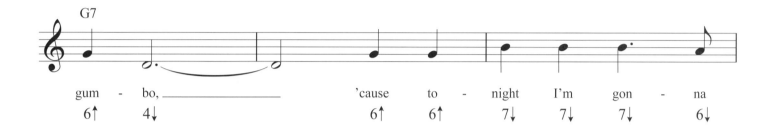

gum - bo, _____ 'cause to - night I'm gon - na

6↑ 4↓ 6↑ 6↑ 7↓ 7↓ 7↓ 6↓

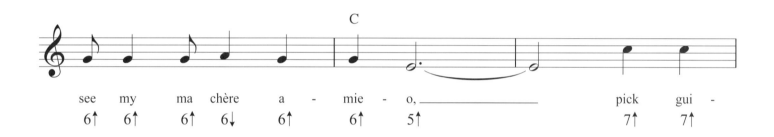

see my ma chère a - mie - o, _____ pick gui -

6↑ 6↑ 6↑ 6↓ 6↑ 6↑ 5↑ 7↑ 7↑

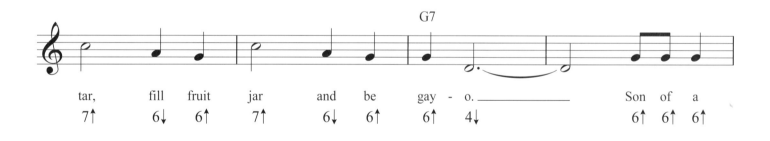

tar, fill fruit jar and be gay - o. _____ Son of a

7↑ 6↓ 6↑ 7↑ 6↓ 6↑ 6↑ 4↓ 6↑ 6↑ 6↑

gun, we'll have big fun on the bay - ou. _____

7↓ 7↓ 6↓ 6↑ 6↓ 6↑ 5↑ 4↓ 4↑

Kum Ba Yah

Traditional Spiritual

C diatonic harmonica

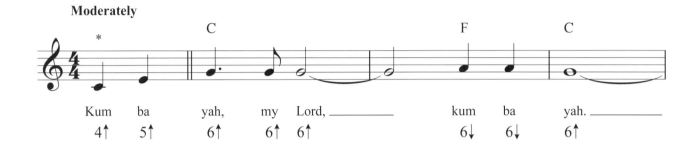

Kum ba yah, my Lord, _____ kum ba yah. _____
4↑ 5↑ 6↑ 6↑ 6↑ 6↓ 6↓ 6↑

_____ Kum ba yah, my Lord, _____ kum ba yah. _____
4↑ 5↑ 6↑ 6↑ 6↑ 5↓ 5↑ 4↓

_____ Kum ba yah, my Lord, _____ kum ba yah. _____
4↑ 5↑ 6↑ 6↑ 6↑ 6↓ 6↓ 6↑

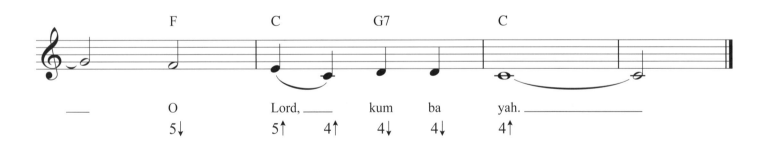

_____ O Lord, _____ kum ba yah. _____
5↓ 5↑ 4↑ 4↓ 4↓ 4↑

*Harmonica sounds one octave higher than written.

Let It Be

Words and Music by John Lennon and Paul McCartney

C diatonic harmonica

*Harmonica sounds one octave higher than written.

Leaving on a Jet Plane

Words and Music by John Denver

C diatonic harmonica

Verse

Moderately

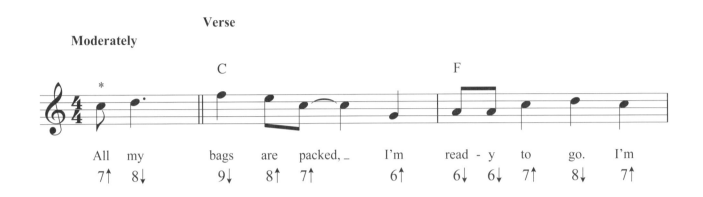

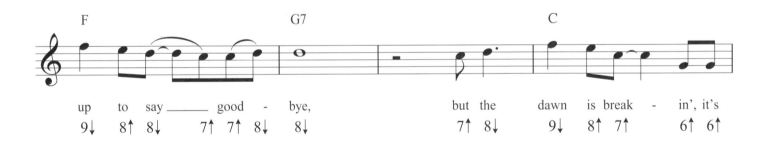

*Harmonica sounds one octave higher than written.

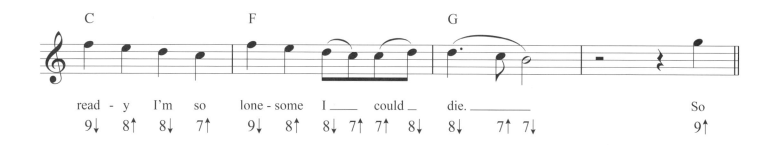

read - y I'm so lone-some I ___ could ___ die. _____ So
9↓ 8↑ 8↓ 7↑ 9↓ 8↑ 8↓ 7↑ 7↑ 8↓ 8↓ 7↑ 7↓ 9↑

Chorus

kiss me and smile for me, ___ tell me that ___ you'll wait for me. ___
9↑ 8↑ 9↑ 9↓ 8↑ 7↑ 9↑ 9↓ 8↑ 9↑ 9↓ 8↑ 7↑

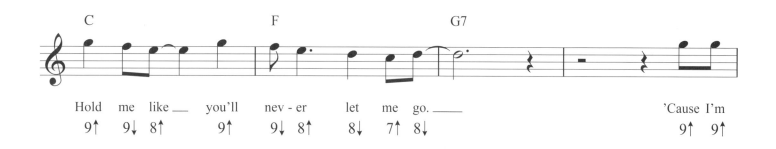

Hold me like ___ you'll nev - er let me go. ____ 'Cause I'm
9↑ 9↓ 8↑ 9↑ 9↓ 8↑ 8↓ 7↑ 8↓ 9↑ 9↑

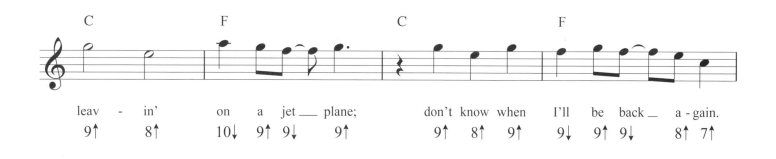

leav - in' on a jet ___ plane; don't know when I'll be back ___ a - gain.
9↑ 8↑ 10↓ 9↑ 9↓ 9↑ 9↑ 8↑ 9↑ 9↓ 9↑ 9↓ 8↑ 7↑

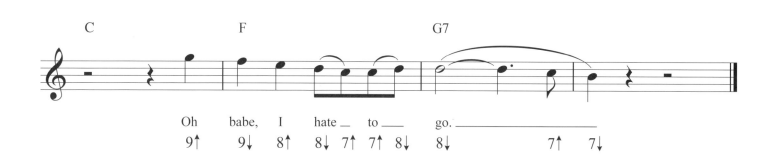

Oh babe, I hate ___ to ___ go. _____
9↑ 9↓ 8↑ 8↓ 7↑ 7↑ 8↓ 8↓ 7↑ 7↓

Love Me Tender

Words and Music by Elvis Presley and Vera Matson

C diatonic harmonica

Verse
Moderately slow

C   D7   G7   C

Love me ten - der, love me sweet, nev - er let me go.
6↑ 7↑ 7↓ 7↑ 8↓ 6↓ 8↓ 7↑ 7↓ 6↓ 7↓ 7↑

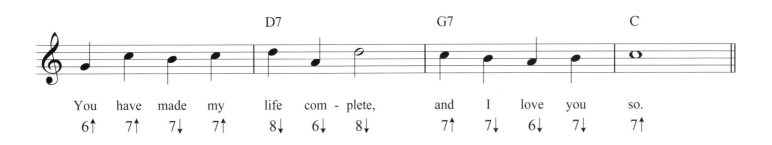

D7   G7   C

You have made my life com - plete, and I love you so.
6↑ 7↑ 7↓ 7↑ 8↓ 6↓ 8↓ 7↑ 7↓ 6↓ 7↓ 7↑

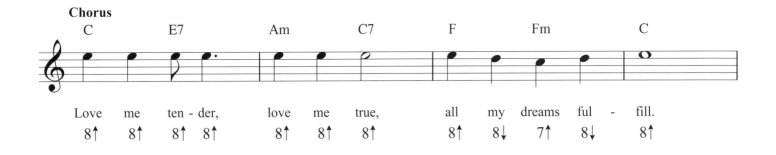

Chorus

C   E7   Am   C7   F   Fm   C

Love me ten - der, love me true, all my dreams ful - fill.
8↑ 8↑ 8↑ 8↑ 8↑ 8↑ 8↑ 8↑ 8↓ 7↑ 8↓ 8↑

A7   D7   G7   C

For, my dar - lin', I love you, and I al - ways will.
8↑ 8↑ 9↓ 8↑ 8↓ 6↓ 8↓ 7↑ 7↓ 6↓ 7↓ 7↑

*Harmonica sounds one octave higher than written.

Michael Row the Boat Ashore

Traditional Folksong

C diatonic harmonica

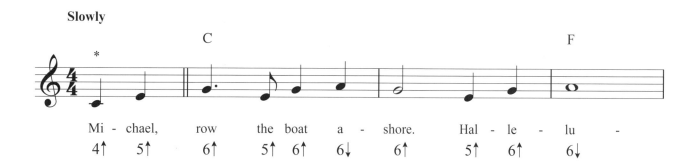

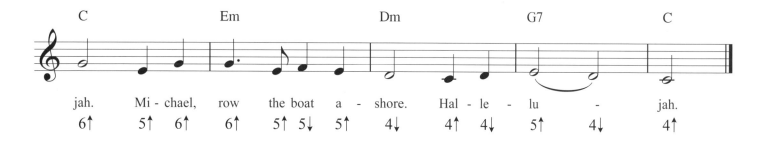

*Harmonica sounds one octave higher than written.

Mr. Bojangles

Words and Music by Jerry Jeff Walker

C diatonic harmonica

*Harmonica sounds one octave higher than written.

Moon River

from the Paramount Picture BREAKFAST AT TIFFANY'S

Words by Johnny Mercer
Music by Henry Mancini

C diatonic harmonica

*Harmonica sounds one octave higher than written.

Morning Has Broken

Words by Eleanor Farjeon
Music by Cat Stevens

C diatonic harmonica

*Harmonica sounds one octave higher than written.

Oh! Susanna

Words and Music by Stephen C. Foster

C diatonic harmonica

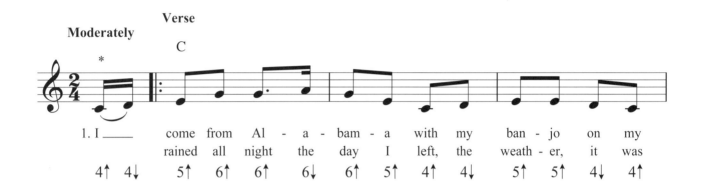

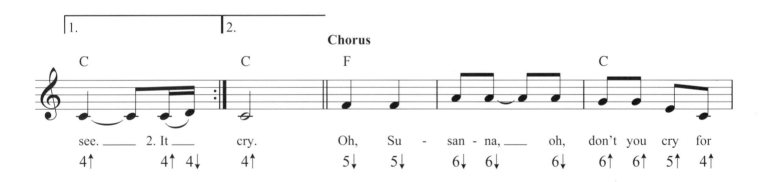

*Harmonica sounds one octave higher than written.

My Girl

Words and Music by William "Smokey" Robinson and Ronald White

C diatonic harmonica

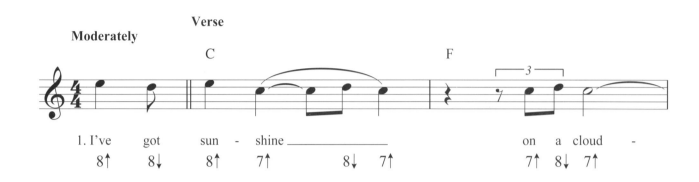

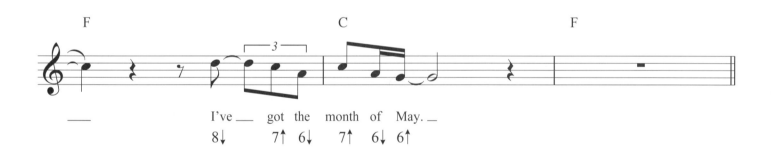

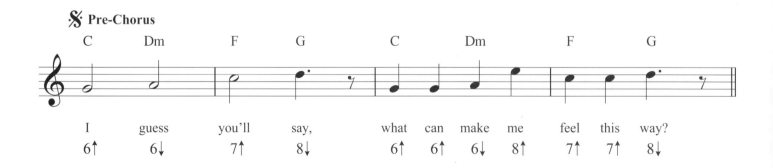

*Harmonica sounds one octave higher than written.

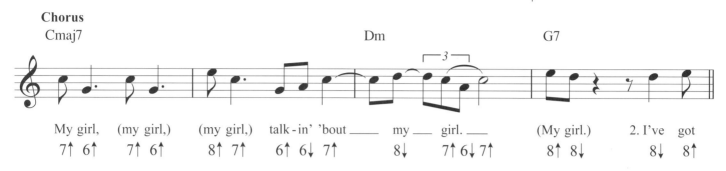

Chorus

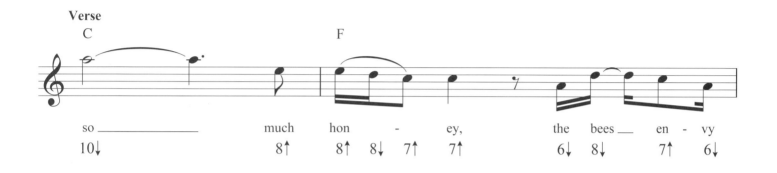

My girl, (my girl,) (my girl,) talk-in' 'bout ____ my ____ girl. (My girl.) 2. I've got
7↑ 6↑ 7↑ 6↑ 8↑ 7↑ 6↑ 6↓ 7↑ 8↓ 7↑ 6↓ 7↑ 8↑ 8↓ 8↓ 8↑

Verse

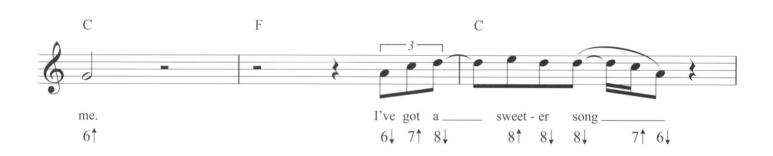

so _____ much hon - ey, the bees ____ en - vy
10↓ 8↑ 8↑ 8↓ 7↑ 7↑ 6↓ 8↓ 7↑ 6↓

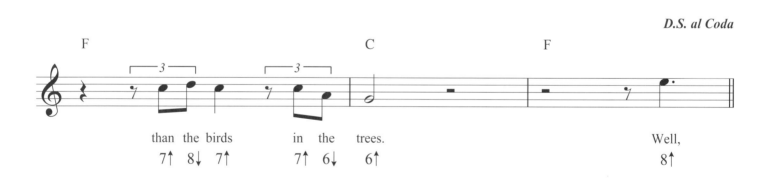

me. I've got a ____ sweet - er song _____
6↑ 6↓ 7↑ 8↓ 8↑ 8↓ 8↓ 7↑ 6↓

D.S. al Coda

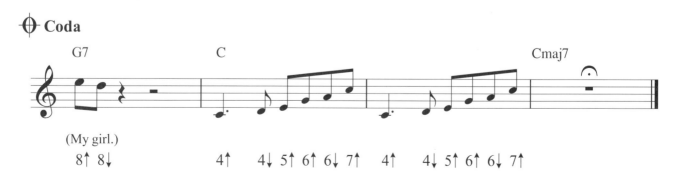

than the birds in the trees. Well,
7↑ 8↓ 7↑ 7↑ 6↓ 6↑ 8↑

Coda

(My girl.)
8↑ 8↓ 4↑ 4↓ 5↑ 6↑ 6↓ 7↑ 4↑ 4↓ 5↑ 6↑ 6↓ 7↑

Ob-La-Di, Ob-La-Da

Words and Music by John Lennon and Paul McCartney

C diatonic harmonica

Verse
Moderately

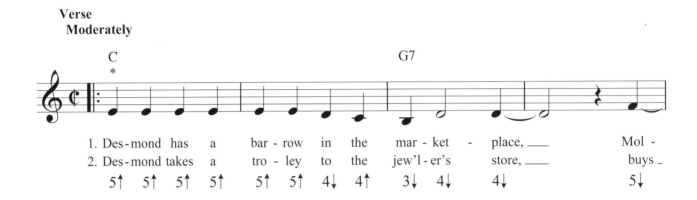

1. Des-mond has a bar-row in the mar-ket - place, ____ Mol-
2. Des-mond takes a tro-ley to the jew'l-er's store, ____ buys

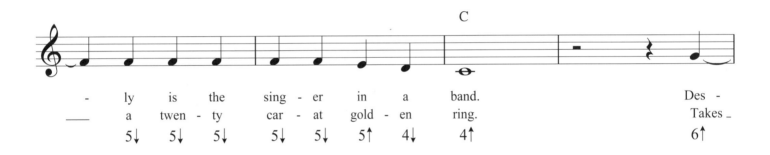

- ly is the sing-er in a band. Des -
 ____ a twen-ty car-at gold-en ring. Takes

- mond says to Mol-ly, "Girl, I like your face," ____ and Mol-ly
 ____ it back to Mol-ly wait-ing at the door, ____ and as he

says this as she takes him by the hand: ____)   "Ob - la - di, ____
gives it to her she be - gins to sing, ____)

*Harmonica sounds one octave higher than written.

Chorus

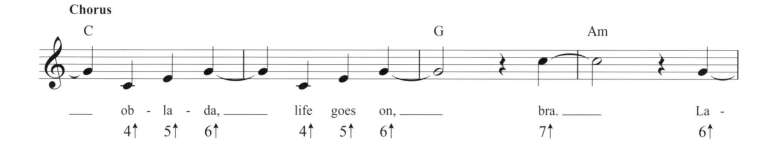

_____ ob - la - da, _____ life goes on, _____ bra. _____ La -

4↑ 5↑ 6↑   4↑ 5↑ 6↑   7↑   6↑

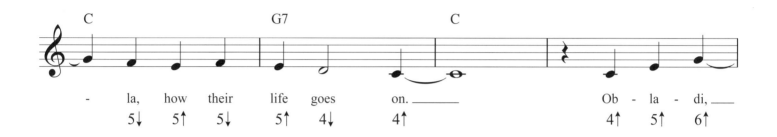

- la, how their life goes on. _____ Ob - la - di, _____

5↓ 5↑ 5↓ 5↑ 4↓ 4↑   4↑ 5↑ 6↑

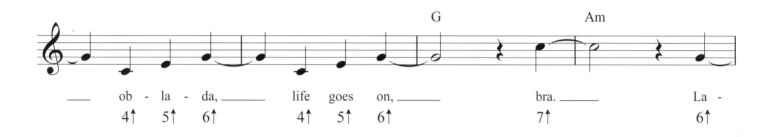

_____ ob - la - da, _____ life goes on, _____ bra. _____ La -

4↑ 5↑ 6↑   4↑ 5↑ 6↑   7↑   6↑

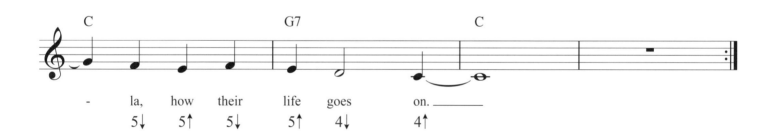

- la, how their life goes on. _____

5↓ 5↑ 5↓ 5↑ 4↓ 4↑

Bridge

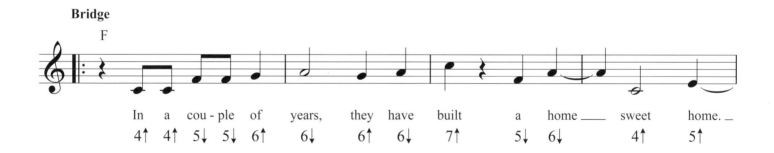

In a cou - ple of years, they have built a home _____ sweet home. _____

4↑ 4↑ 5↓ 5↓ 6↑ 6↓ 6↑ 6↓ 7↑ 5↓ 6↓ 4↑ 5↑

_____

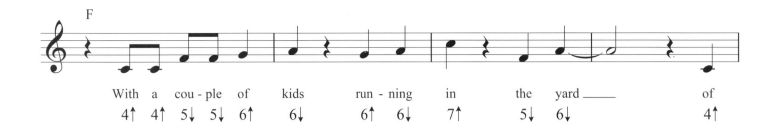

With a cou - ple of kids run - ning in the yard ____ of

4↑ 4↑ 5↓ 5↓ 6↑ 6↓ 6↑ 6↓ 7↑ 5↓ 6↓ 4↑

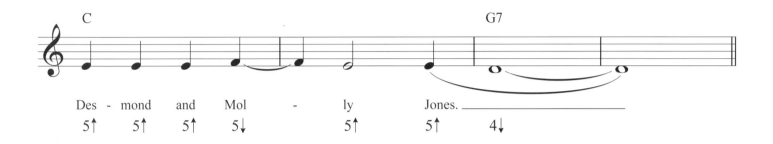

Des - mond and Mol - ly Jones. _____

5↑ 5↑ 5↑ 5↓ 5↑ 5↑ 4↓

Verse

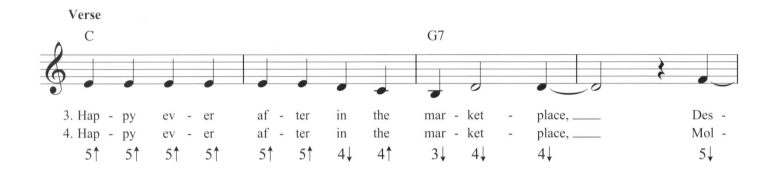

3. Hap - py ev - er af - ter in the mar - ket - place, ___ Des -
4. Hap - py ev - er af - ter in the mar - ket - place, ___ Mol -

5↑ 5↑ 5↑ 5↑ 5↑ 5↑ 4↓ 4↑ 3↓ 4↓ 4↓ 5↓

- mond lets the chil - dren lend a hand. Mol -
- ly lets the chil - dren lend a hand. Des -

5↓ 5↓ 5↓ 5↓ 5↓ 5↑ 4↓ 4↑ 6↑

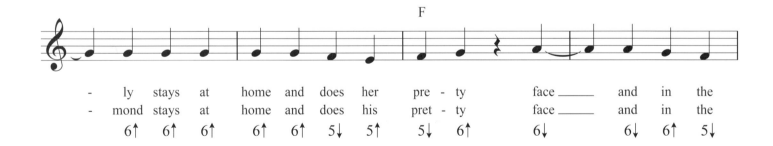

- ly stays at home and does her pre - ty face ____ and in the
- mond stays at home and does his pret - ty face ____ and in the

6↑ 6↑ 6↑ 6↑ 6↑ 5↓ 5↑ 5↓ 6↑ 6↓ 6↓ 6↑ 5↓

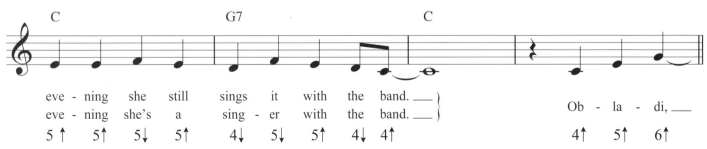

eve - ning she still sings it with the band. __ }
eve - ning she's a sing - er with the band. __ }

Ob - la - di, __

5↑ 5↑ 5↓ 5↑ 4↓ 5↓ 5↑ 4↓ 4↑ 4↑ 5↑ 6↑

44

Chorus

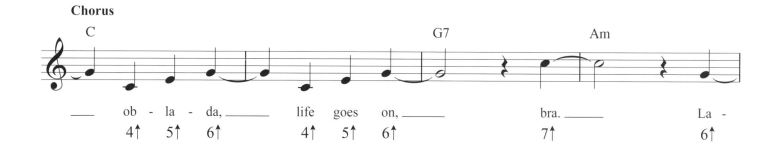

—— ob - la - da, ——— life goes on, ——— bra. ——— La -
4↑ 5↑ 6↑   4↑ 5↑ 6↑   7↑   6↑

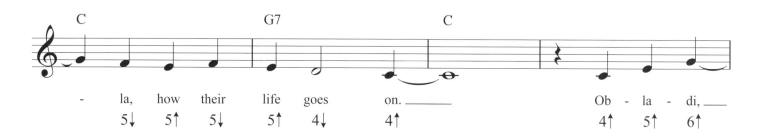

- la, how their life goes on. ——— Ob - la - di, ———
5↓ 5↑ 5↓ 5↑ 4↓ 4↑   4↑ 5↑ 6↑

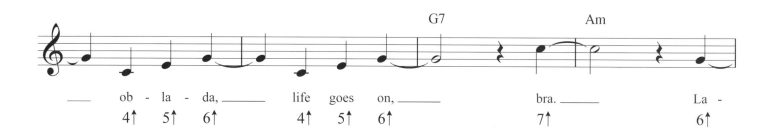

—— ob - la - da, ——— life goes on, ——— bra. ——— La -
4↑ 5↑ 6↑   4↑ 5↑ 6↑   7↑   6↑

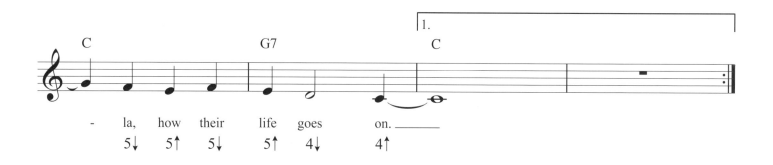

1.

- la, how their life goes on. ———
5↓ 5↑ 5↓ 5↑ 4↓ 4↑

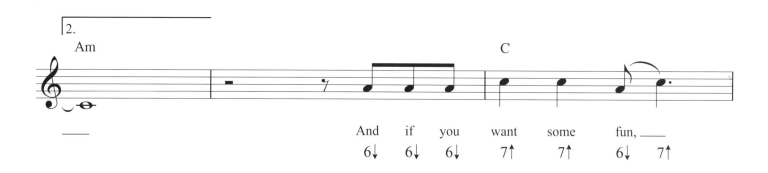

2.

And if you want some fun, ———
6↓ 6↓ 6↓ 7↑ 7↑ 6↓ 7↑

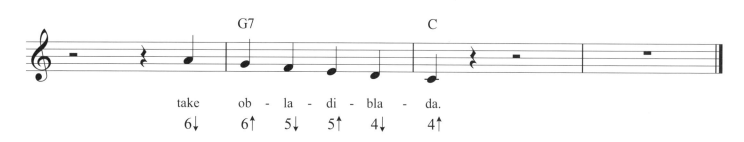

take ob - la - di - bla - da.
6↓ 6↑ 5↓ 5↑ 4↓ 4↑

Puff the Magic Dragon

Words and Music by Lenny Lipton and Peter Yarrow

C diatonic harmonica

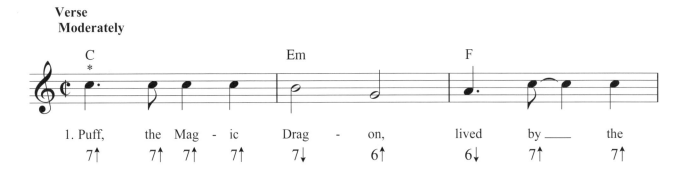

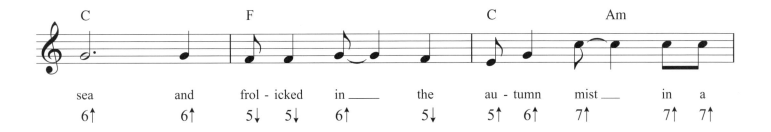

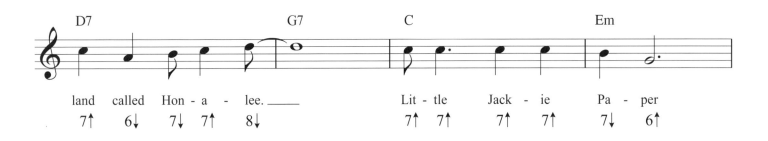

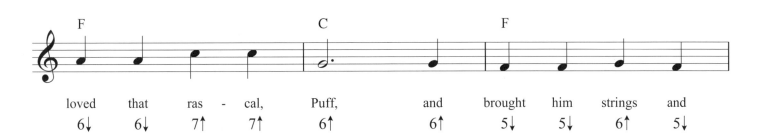

*Harmonica sounds one octave higher than written.

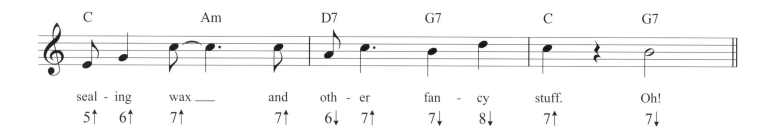

seal - ing wax ___ and oth - er fan - cy stuff. Oh!
5↑ 6↑ 7↑ 7↑ 6↓ 7↑ 7↓ 8↓ 7↑ 7↓

Verse

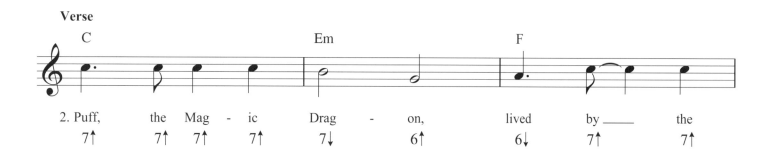

2. Puff, the Mag - ic Drag - on, lived by ___ the
7↑ 7↑ 7↑ 7↑ 7↓ 6↑ 6↓ 7↑ 7↑

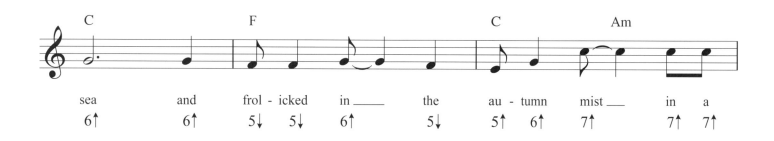

sea and frol - icked in ___ the au - tumn mist ___ in a
6↑ 6↑ 5↓ 5↓ 6↑ 5↓ 5↑ 6↑ 7↑ 7↑ 7↑

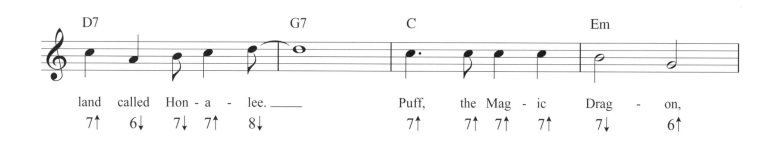

land called Hon - a - lee. ___ Puff, the Mag - ic Drag - on,
7↑ 6↓ 7↓ 7↑ 8↓ 7↑ 7↑ 7↑ 7↑ 7↓ 6↑

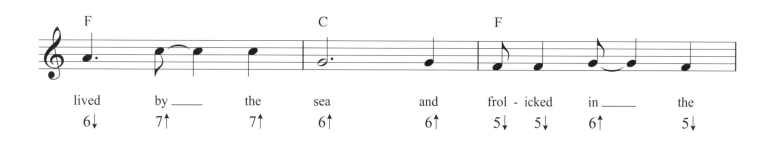

lived by ___ the sea and frol - icked in ___ the
6↓ 7↑ 7↑ 6↑ 6↑ 5↓ 5↓ 6↑ 5↓

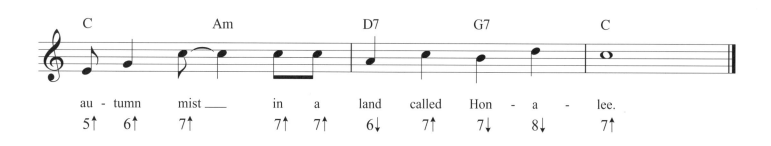

au - tumn mist ___ in a land called Hon - a - lee.
5↑ 6↑ 7↑ 7↑ 7↑ 6↓ 7↑ 7↓ 8↓ 7↑

Ring of Fire

Words and Music by Merle Kilgore and June Carter

C diatonic harmonica

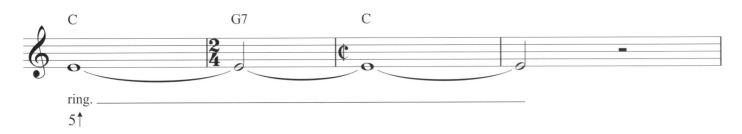

*Harmonica sounds one octave higher then written.

Bound _____ by wild de - sire, _____
6↑   6↑ 6↓ 5↓ 6↑

_____   I fell in - to a ring of
                        5↑ 5↑ 5↑   5↑ 5↑ 5↓ 4↓

Chorus

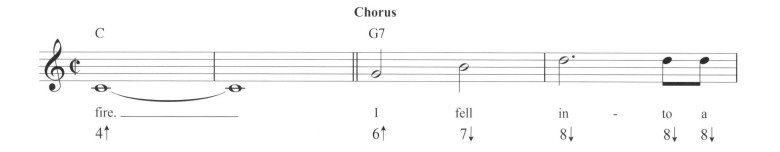

fire. _____ I   fell   in - to   a
4↑   6↑   7↓   8↓   8↓ 8↓

burn - ing ring   of   fire. ___ I went down, down, down   and the
7↑   7↑   7↑   7↑   6↓   6↑   6↑ 6↑   6↑   7↓   8↓   8↓ 8↓

flames went   high - er. And it burns, burns,   burns, _____
7↑   7↑   6↓   6↑   5↑ 4↓ 4↑   5↑   6↑

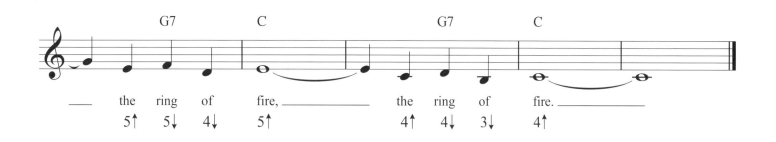

___ the ring   of   fire, _____   the ring   of   fire. _____
5↑ 5↓   4↓   5↑   4↑   4↓ 3↓   4↑

Scarborough Fair

Traditional English

C diatonic harmonica

Moderately

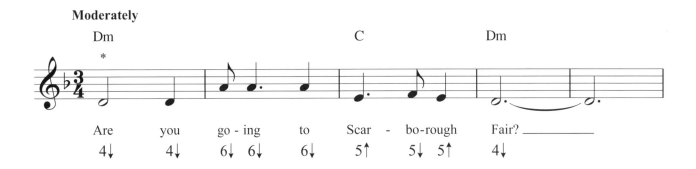

Are you go-ing to Scar - bo-rough Fair? _____
4↓ 4↓ 6↓ 6↓ 6↓ 5↑ 5↓ 5↑ 4↓

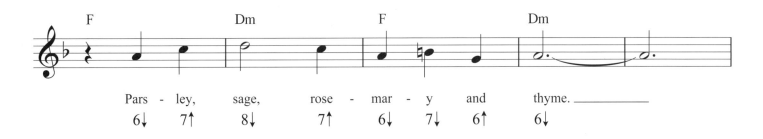

Pars - ley, sage, rose - mar - y and thyme. _____
6↓ 7↑ 8↓ 7↑ 6↓ 7↓ 6↑ 6↓

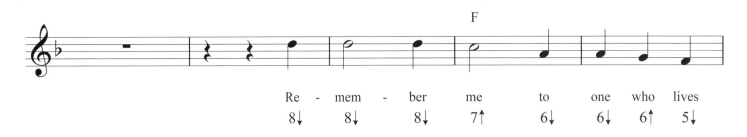

Re - mem - ber me to one who lives
8↓ 8↓ 8↓ 7↑ 6↓ 6↓ 6↑ 5↓

there. _____ She once was a
5↑ 4↑ 4↓ 6↓ 6↑ 5↓

true love of mine. _____
5↑ 4↓ 4↑ 4↓

*Harmonica sounds one octave higher than written.

The Sound of Silence

Words and Music by Paul Simon

C diatonic harmonica

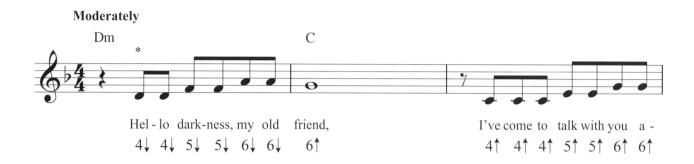

Hel - lo dark-ness, my old friend,
4↓ 4↓ 5↓ 5↓ 6↓ 6↓ 6↑

I've come to talk with you a -
4↑ 4↑ 4↑ 5↑ 5↑ 6↑ 6↑

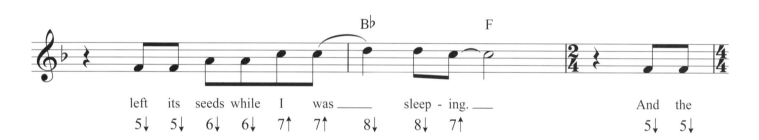

gain,
5↓

be - cause a vi - sion soft - ly _____ creep - ing _____
5↓ 5↓ 5↓ 6↓ 6↓ 7↑ 7↑ 8↓ 8↓ 7↑

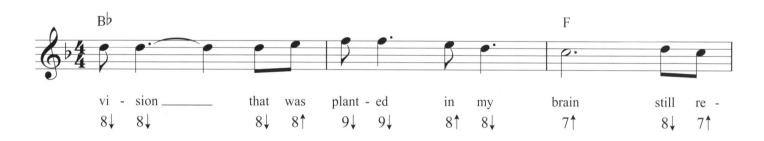

left its seeds while I was _____ sleep - ing. _____ And the
5↓ 5↓ 6↓ 6↓ 7↑ 7↑ 8↓ 8↓ 7↑ 5↓ 5↓

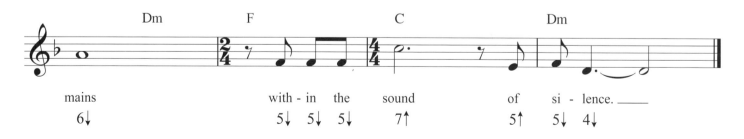

vi - sion _____ that was plant - ed in my brain still re -
8↓ 8↓ 8↓ 8↑ 9↓ 9↓ 8↑ 8↓ 7↑ 8↓ 7↑

mains
6↓

with - in the sound of si - lence.
5↓ 5↓ 5↓ 7↑ 5↑ 5↓ 4↓

*Harmonica sounds one octave higher than written.

So Long It's Been Good To Know Yuh

(Dusty Old Dust)

Words and Music by Woody Guthrie

C diatonic harmonica

Verse

Moderately

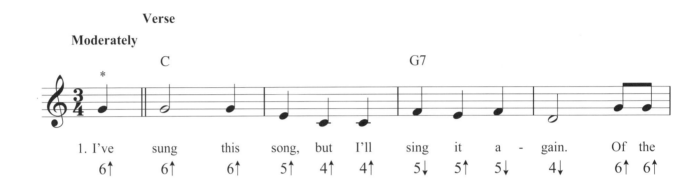

1. I've sung this song, but I'll sing it a - gain. Of the
6↑ 6↑ 6↑ 5↑ 4↑ 4↑ 5↓ 5↑ 5↓ 4↓ 6↑ 6↑

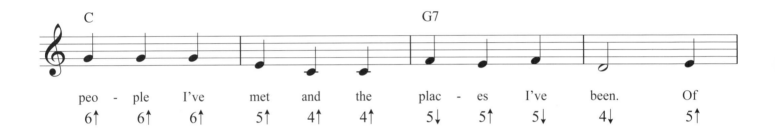

peo - ple I've met and the plac - es I've been. Of
6↑ 6↑ 6↑ 5↑ 4↑ 4↑ 5↓ 5↑ 5↓ 4↓ 5↑

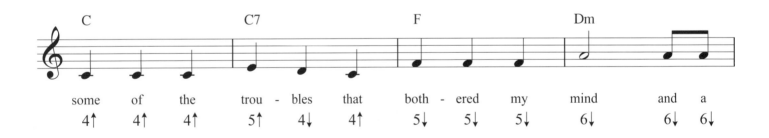

some of the trou - bles that both - ered my mind and a
4↑ 4↑ 4↑ 5↑ 4↓ 4↑ 5↓ 5↓ 5↓ 6↓ 6↓ 6↓

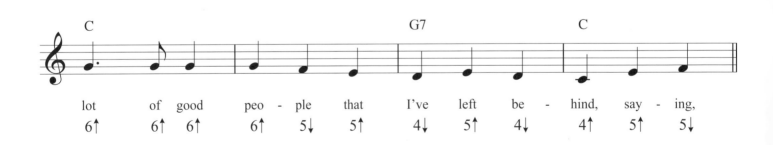

lot of good peo - ple that I've left be - hind, say - ing,
6↑ 6↑ 6↑ 6↑ 5↓ 5↑ 4↓ 5↑ 4↓ 4↑ 5↑ 5↓

*Harmonica sounds one octave higher than written.

Chorus

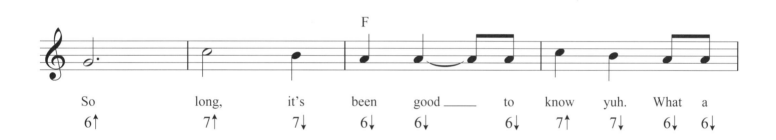

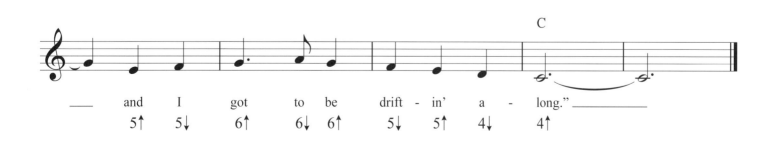

Stand by Me

Words and Music by Jerry Leiber, Mike Stoller and Ben E. King

C diatonic harmonica

*Harmonica sounds one octave higher than written.

see.

4↑

Oh, I won't

5↑ 6↑ 6↓

be a - fraid.

5↑ 6↑ 6↓

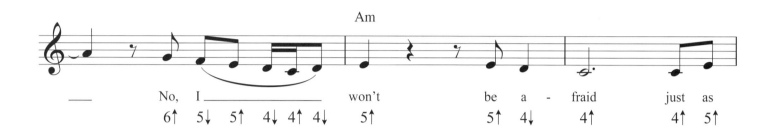

Am

No, I won't

6↑ 5↓ 5↑ 4↓ 4↑ 4↓ 5↑

be a - fraid

5↑ 4↓ 4↑

just as

4↑ 5↑

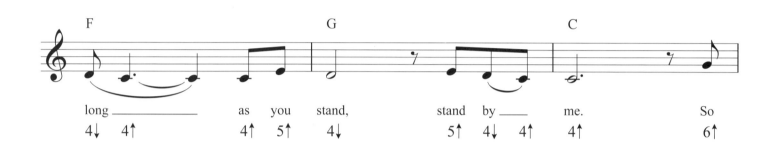

F

long as you stand,

4↓ 4↑ 4↑ 5↑ 4↓

G

stand by me.

5↑ 4↓ 4↑ 4↑

C

So

6↑

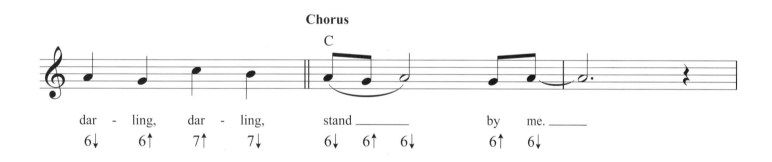

Chorus

C

dar - ling, dar - ling,

6↓ 6↑ 7↑ 7↓

stand by me.

6↓ 6↑ 6↓ 6↑ 6↓

Am

Stand by me.

5↑ 4↑ 4↓ 4↑

Oh, stand,

5↑ 4↓ 4↑

F

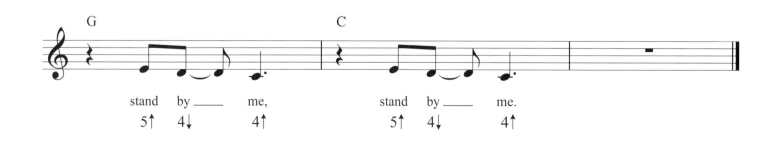

G

stand by me,

5↑ 4↓ 4↑

C

stand by me.

5↑ 4↓ 4↑

Summertime
from PORGY AND BESS ®

Music and Lyrics by George Gershwin, DuBose and Dorothy Heyward and Ira Gershwin

C diatonic harmonica

*Harmonica sounds one octave higher than written.

Sweet Caroline

Words and Music by Neil Diamond

C diatonic harmonica

*Harmonica sounds one octave higher than written.

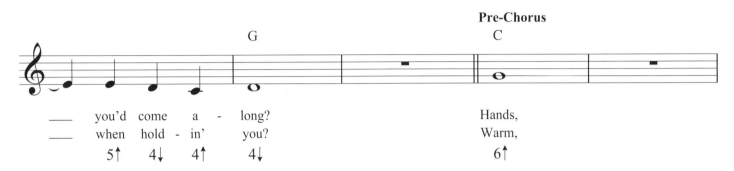

Pre-Chorus

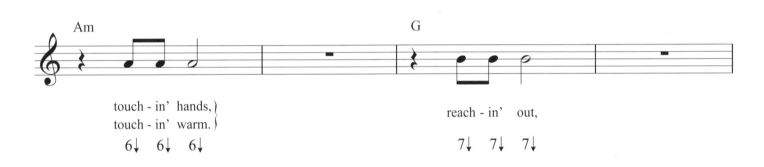

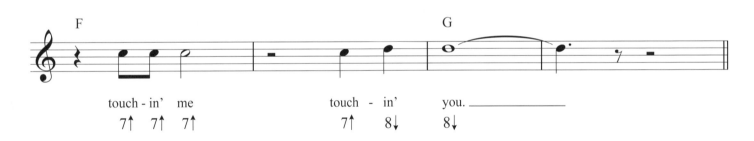

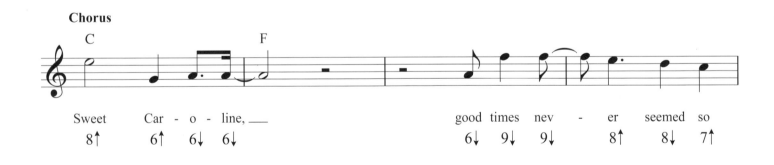

Chorus

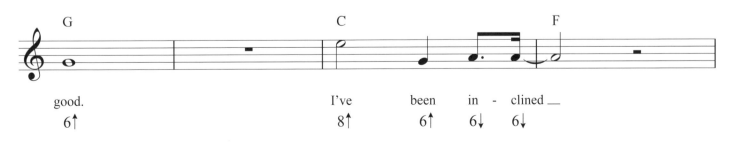

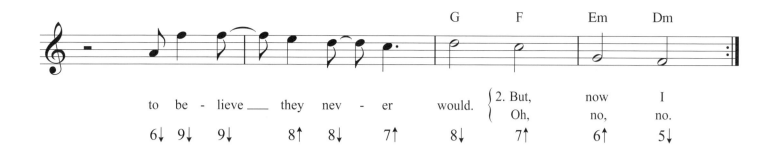

to be - lieve ___ they nev - er would. { 2. But,   now   I
                                          Oh,   no,   no.
6↓ 9↓ 9↓   8↑ 8↓ 7↑   8↓   7↑   6↑   5↓

Interlude

4↓ 5↑ 5↓   4↓ 5↑ 5↓ 5↑ 4↓   5↓ 5↑ 4↓   5↓ 6↑ 6↓   5↓ 6↑

6↓ 6↑ 5↓   6↓ 6↑ 5↓   6↓ 7↓ 7↑   6↓ 7↓ 7↑   7↓   8↑   8↓

Chorus

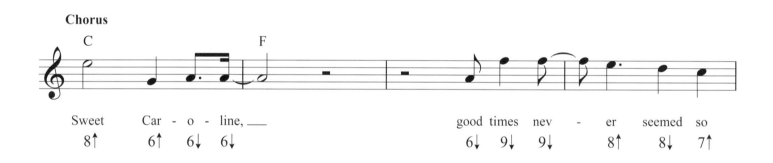

Sweet   Car - o - line, ___   good times nev - er seemed so
8↑   6↑ 6↓ 6↓   6↓ 9↓ 9↓   8↑ 8↓ 7↑

good.   I've   been in - clined ___   to be - lieve ___
6↑   8↑   6↑ 6↓ 6↓   6↓ 9↓ 9↓

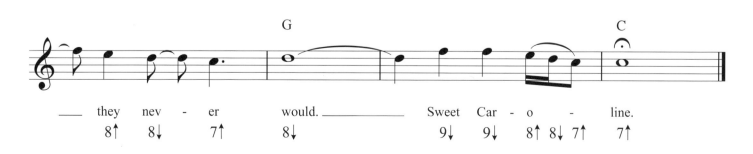

___ they nev - er   would. _____ Sweet Car - o - line.
8↑ 8↓ 7↑   8↓   9↓ 9↓ 8↑ 8↓ 7↑ 7↑

This Land Is Your Land

Words and Music by Woody Guthrie

C diatonic harmonica

Moderately

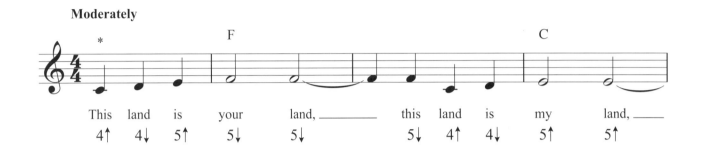

This land is your land, _____ this land is my land, _____
4↑ 4↓ 5↑ 5↓ 5↓ 5↓ 4↑ 4↓ 5↑ 5↑

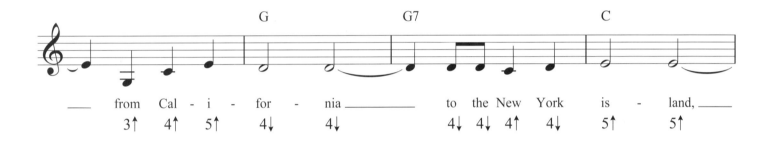

_____ from Cal - i - for - nia _____ to the New York is - land, _____
3↑ 4↑ 5↑ 4↓ 4↓ 4↓ 4↓ 4↑ 4↓ 5↑ 5↑

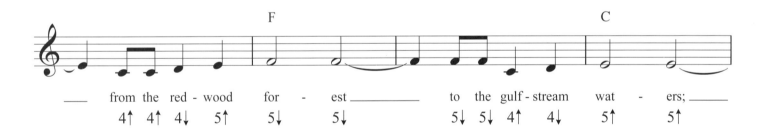

_____ from the red - wood for - est _____ to the gulf - stream wat - ers; _____
4↑ 4↑ 4↓ 5↑ 5↓ 5↓ 5↓ 5↓ 4↑ 4↓ 5↑ 5↑

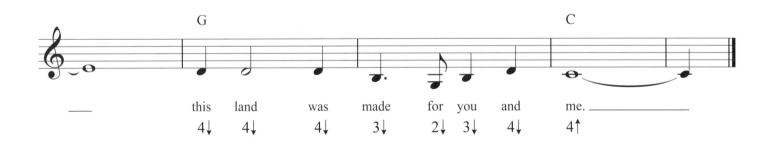

_____ this land was made for you and me. _____
4↓ 4↓ 4↓ 3↓ 2↓ 3↓ 4↓ 4↑

*Harmonica sounds one octave higher than written.

Take Me Home, Country Roads

Words and Music by John Denver, Bill Danoff and Taffy Nivert

C diatonic harmonica

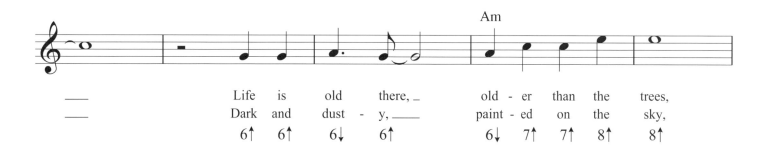

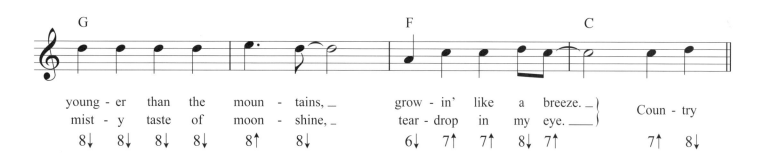

*Harmonica sounds one octave higher than written.

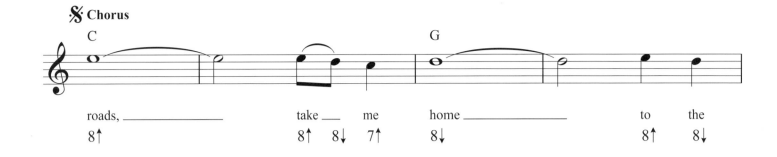

§ Chorus

C   G

roads, _____ take __ me home _____ to the

8↑   8↑ 8↓ 7↑   8↓   8↑   8↓

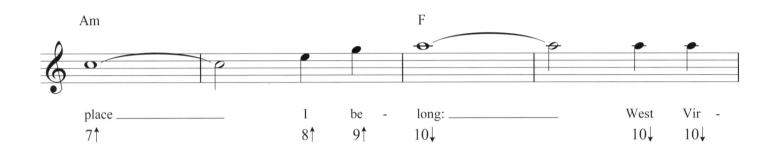

Am   F

place _____ I be - long: _____ West Vir -

7↑   8↑ 9↑ 10↓   10↓ 10↓

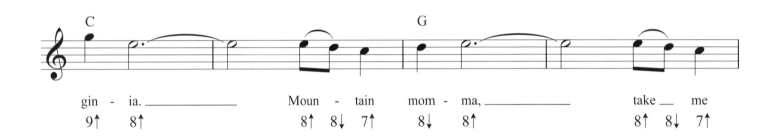

C   G

gin - ia. _____ Moun - tain mom - ma, _____ take __ me

9↑ 8↑   8↑ 8↓ 7↑   8↓ 8↑   8↑ 8↓ 7↑

To Coda ⊕

F   C

home, _____ coun - try roads. _____

7↑   7↑ 8↓ 7↑

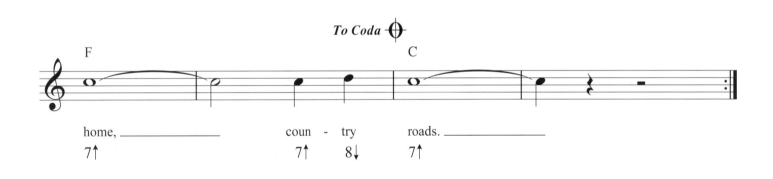

Bridge

Am   G   C

I hear her voice in the morn - in' hours, she

7↑ 7↑ 7↑ 7↓   7↑ 8↓ 8↑ 8↑ 8↑ 8↑

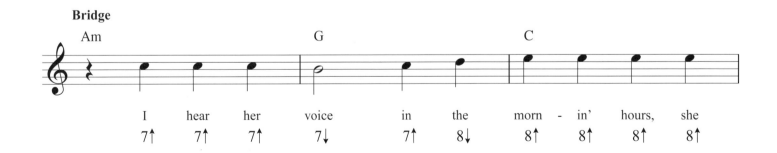

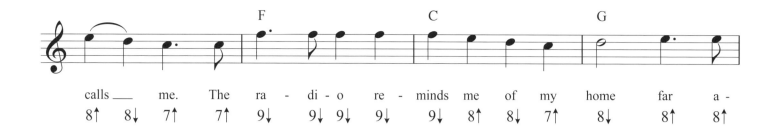

calls ___ me. The ra - di - o re - minds me of my home far a -
8↑ 8↓ 7↑   7↑ 9↓ 9↓ 9↓ 9↓ 9↓ 8↑ 8↓ 7↑ 8↓   8↑ 8↑

way.   And driv - in' down the road I get a feel - in' that I
8↓   8↓   8↑ 8↑   8↑   8↑   8↓ 8↓ 8↓ 8↓   7↑   7↑ 7↑ 7↑

D.S. al Coda

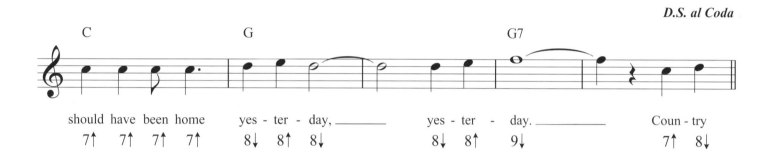

should have been home yes - ter - day, _____ yes - ter - day. _____ Coun - try
7↑ 7↑ 7↑ 7↑   8↓ 8↑ 8↓   8↓ 8↑ 9↓   7↑ 8↓

⊕ Coda

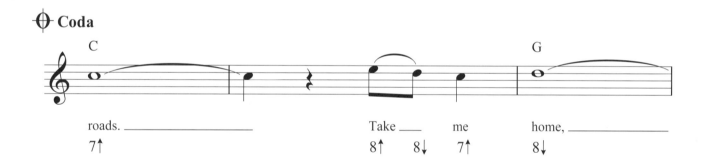

roads. _____   Take ___ me home, _____
7↑   8↑   8↓ 7↑   8↓

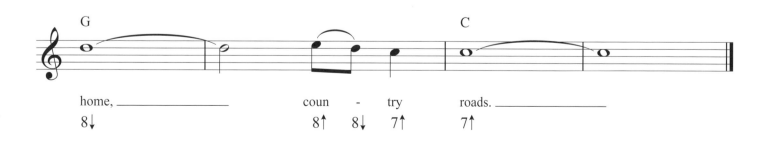

___   coun - try roads. _____   Take ___ me
         8↑ 8↓ 7↑   7↑   8↑   8↓ 7↑

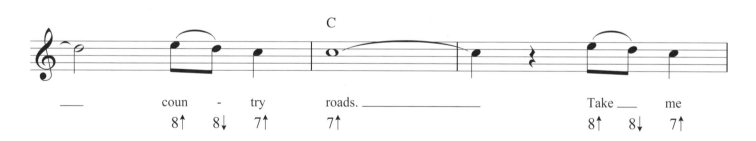

home, _____   coun - try roads. _____
8↓   8↑   8↓ 7↑   7↑

The Times They Are A-Changin'

Words and Music by Bob Dylan

C diatonic harmonica

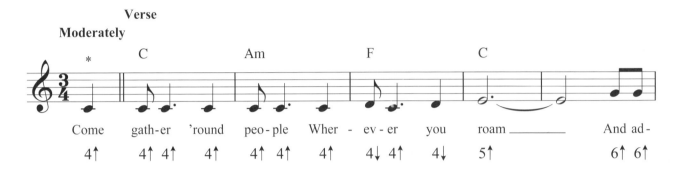

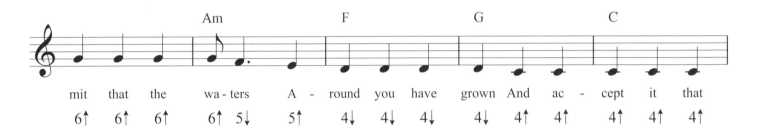

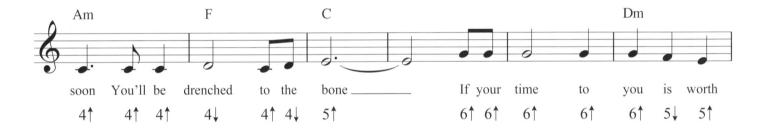

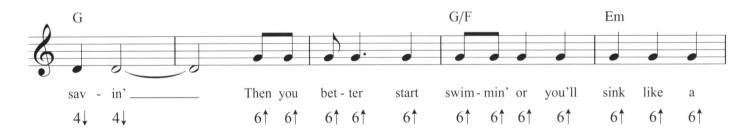

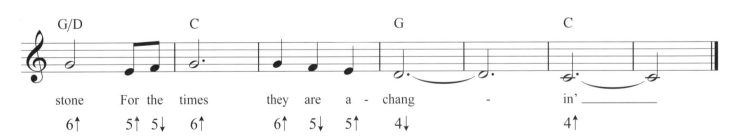

*Harmonica sounds one octave higher than written.

Tom Dooley

Words and Music Collected, Adapted and Arranged by
Frank Warner, John A. Lomax and Alan Lomax
From the singing of Frank Proffitt

C diatonic harmonica

Moderately

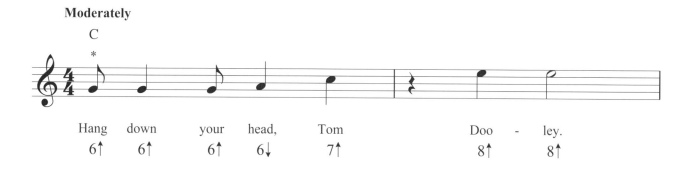

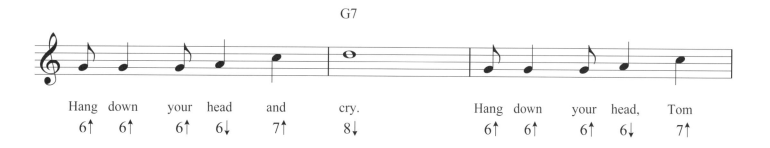

*Harmonica sounds one octave higher than written.

Turn! Turn! Turn!
(To Everything There Is a Season)

Words from the Book of Ecclesiastes
Adaptation and Music by Pete Seeger

C diatonic harmonica

*Harmonica sounds one octave higher than written.

When I Grow Too Old to Dream

Lyrics by Oscar Hammerstein II
Music by Sigmund Romberg

C diatonic harmonica

What a Wonderful World

Words and Music by George David Weiss and Bob Thiele

C diatonic harmonica

*Harmonica sounds one octave higher than written.

Bridge

col-ors of the rain-bow, so pret-ty in the sky, are al-so on the fac-es of

4↓ 4↓ 4↓ 4↓ 4↓ 3↑ 3↑ 5↓ 5↑ 5↑ 4↓ 5↑ 4↑ 4↓ 4↓ 4↓ 4↓ 4↓ 3↑ 4↓

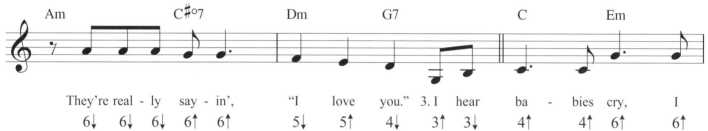

peo-ple go-in' by. I see friends shak-in' hands, ___ say-in', "How do you do?"

5↓ 5↑ 5↑ 4↓ 5↑ 5↑ 6↑ 6↓ 6↓ 6↓ 6↑ 5↑ 6↑ 6↓ 6↓ 6↓ 6↑

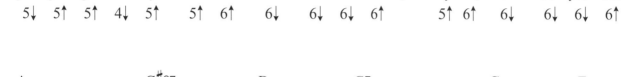

They're real-ly say-in', "I love you." 3. I hear ba-bies cry, I

6↓ 6↓ 6↓ 6↑ 6↑ 5↓ 5↑ 4↓ 3↑ 3↓ 4↑ 4↑ 6↑ 6↑

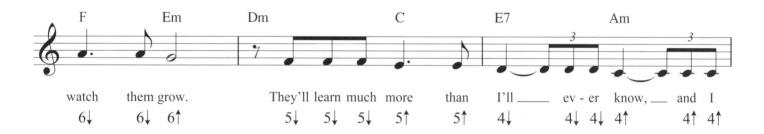

watch them grow. They'll learn much more than I'll ___ ev-er know, ___ and I

6↓ 6↓ 6↑ 5↓ 5↓ 5↓ 5↑ 5↑ 4↓ 4↓ 4↓ 4↑ 4↑ 4↑

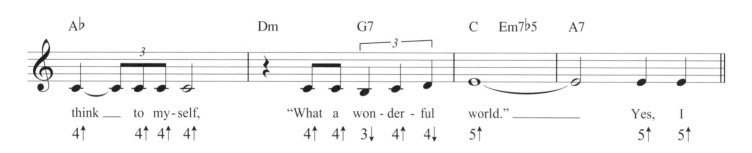

think ___ to my-self, "What a won-der-ful world." _____ Yes, I

4↑ 4↑ 4↑ 4↑ 4↑ 4↑ 3↓ 4↑ 4↓ 5↑ 5↑ 5↑

Outro

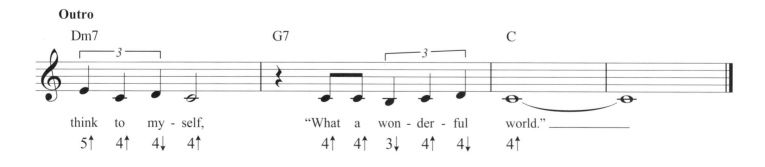

think to my-self, "What a won-der-ful world." _____

5↑ 4↑ 4↓ 4↑ 4↑ 4↑ 3↓ 4↑ 4↓ 4↑

When Irish Eyes Are Smiling

Words by Chauncey Olcott and George Graff, Jr.
Music by Ernest R. Ball

C diatonic harmonica

*Harmonica sounds one octave higher than written.

When the Saints Go Marching In

Words by Katherine E. Purvis
Music by James M. Black

C diatonic harmonica

Moderately

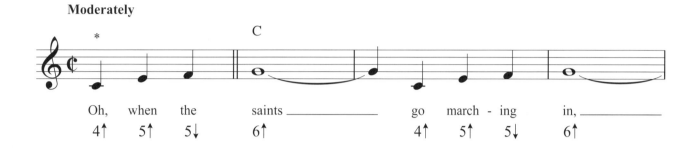

Oh, when the saints go march - ing in,
4↑ 5↑ 5↓ 6↑ 4↑ 5↑ 5↓ 6↑

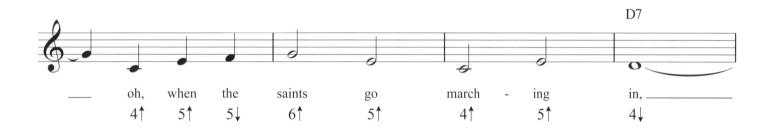

oh, when the saints go march - ing in,
4↑ 5↑ 5↓ 6↑ 5↑ 4↑ 5↑ 4↓

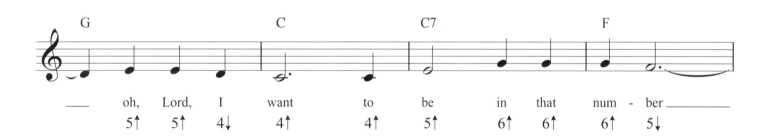

oh, Lord, I want to be in that num - ber
5↑ 5↑ 4↓ 4↑ 4↑ 5↑ 6↑ 6↑ 6↑ 5↓

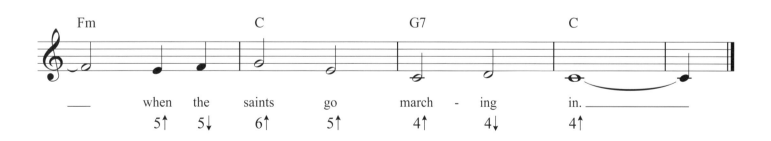

when the saints go march - ing in.
5↑ 5↓ 6↑ 5↑ 4↑ 4↓ 4↑

*Harmonica sounds one octave higher than written.

With a Little Help from My Friends

Words and Music by John Lennon and Paul McCartney

C diatonic harmonica

*Harmonica sounds one octave higher than written.

Chorus

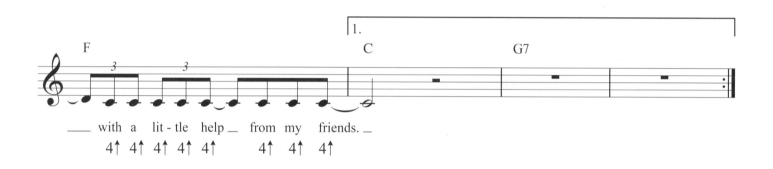

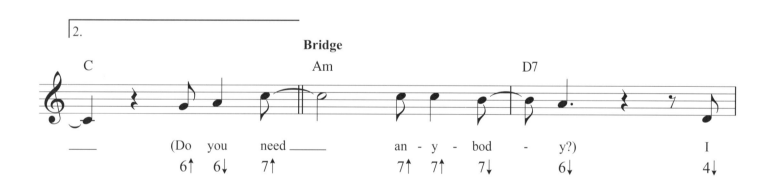

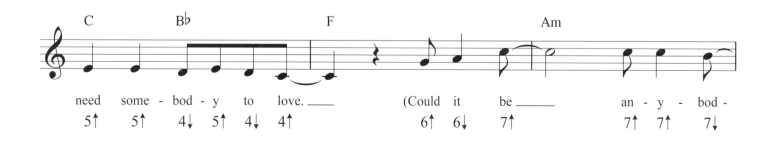

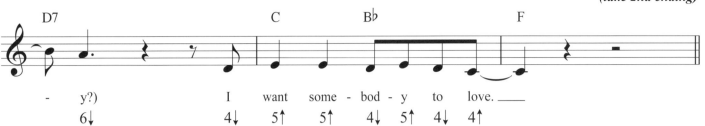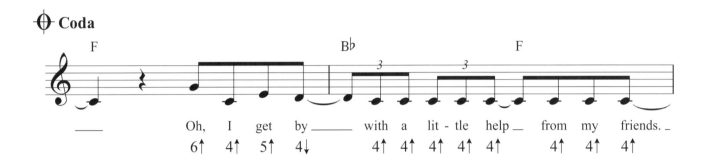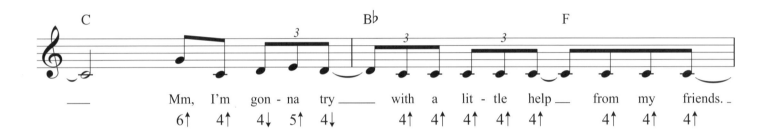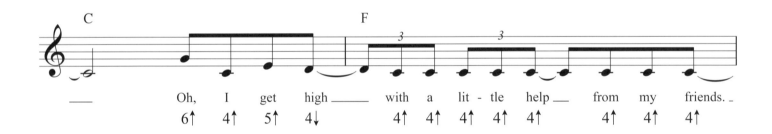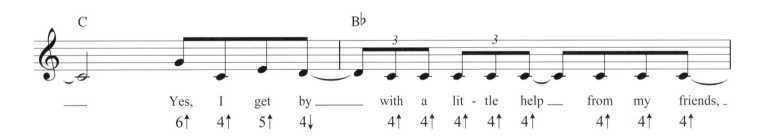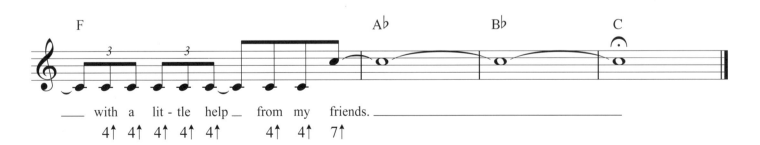

You Are My Sunshine

Words and Music by Jimmie Davis

C diatonic harmonica

*Harmonica sounds one octave higher than written.

You Gotta Move

Words and Music by Fred McDowell and Gary Davis

C diatonic harmonica

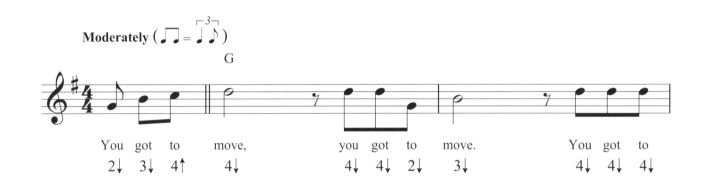

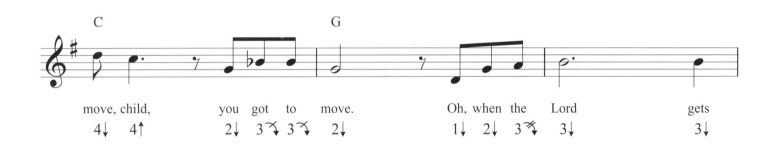

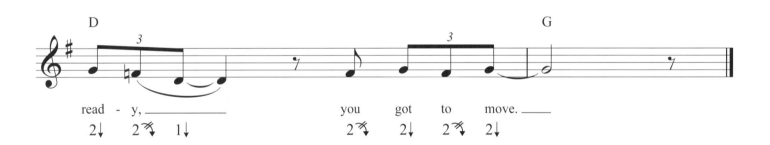

Your Cheatin' Heart

Words and Music by Hank Williams

C diatonic harmonica

HARMONICA NOTATION LEGEND

Harmonica music can be notated two different ways: on a *musical staff*, and in *tablature*.

THE MUSICAL STAFF shows pitches and rhythms and is divided by bar lines into measures. Pitches are named after the first seven letters of the alphabet.

TABLATURE graphically represents the harmonica music. Each note will be accompanied by a number, 1 through 10, indicating what hole you are to play. The arrow that follows indicates whether to blow or draw. (All examples are shown using a C diatonic harmonica.)

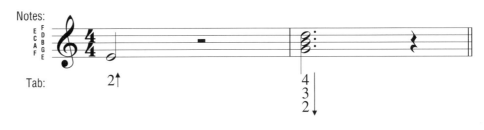

Notes:

Tab:

Blow (exhale) into 2nd hole.

Draw (inhale) 2nd, 3rd, & 4th holes together.

Notes on the C Harmonica

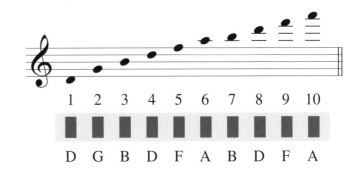

Exhaled (Blown) Notes

1	2	3	4	5	6	7	8	9	10
C	E	G	C	E	G	C	E	G	C

Inhaled (Drawn) Notes

1	2	3	4	5	6	7	8	9	10
D	G	B	D	F	A	B	D	F	A

Bends

Blow Bends

- 1/4 step
- 1/2 step
- 1 step
- 1 1/2 steps

Draw Bends

- 1/4 step
- 1/2 step
- 1 step
- 1 1/2 steps

Definitions for Special Harmonica Notation

SLURRED BEND: Play (draw) 3rd hole, then bend the note down one whole step.

GRACE NOTE BEND: Starting with a pre-bent note, immediately release bend to the target note.

VIBRATO: Begin adding vibrato to the sustained note on beat 3.

TONGUE BLOCKING: Using your tongue to block holes 2 & 3, play octaves on holes 1 & 4.

NOTE: Tablature numbers in parentheses are used when:
- The note is sustained, but a new articulation begins (such as vibrato), or
- The quantity of notes being sustained changes, or
- A change in dynamics (volume) occurs.

Additional Musical Definitions

D.S. al Coda
- Go back to the sign (𝄋), then play until the measure marked "***To Coda***," then skip to the section labelled "**Coda**."

D.C. al Fine
- Go back to the beginning of the song and play until the measure marked "***Fine***" (end).

- Repeat measures between signs.

(accent)
- Accentuate the note (play initial attack louder).

(staccato)
- Play the note short.

- When a repeated section has different endings, play the first ending only the first time and the second ending only the second time.

Dynamics

p • Piano (soft)

mp • Mezzo Piano (medium soft)

mf • Mezzo Forte (medium loud)

f • Forte (loud)

(crescendo) • Gradually louder

(decrescendo) • Gradually softer

HAL·LEONARD® HARMONICA PLAY-ALONG

Play your favorite songs quickly and easily!

Just follow the notation, listen to the audio to hear how the harmonica should sound, and then play along using the separate full-band backing tracks. The melody and lyrics are also included in the book in case you want to sing, or to simply help you follow along. The audio includes playback tools so you can adjust the recording to any tempo without changing pitch!

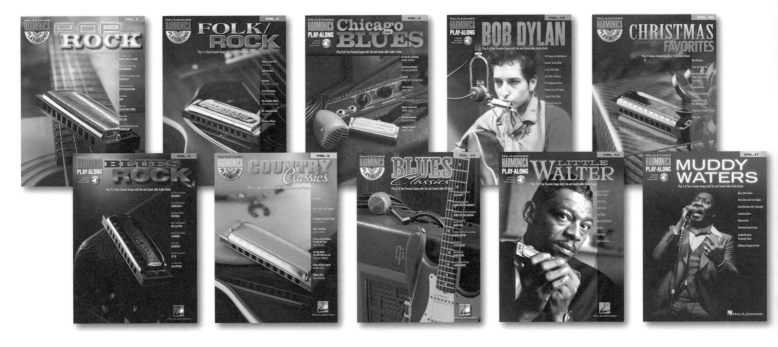

1. Pop/Rock
And When I Die • Bright Side of the Road • I Should Have Known Better • Low Rider • Miss You • Piano Man • Take the Long Way Home • You Don't Know How It Feels.
00000478 Book/CD Pack $16.99

2. Rock Hits
Cowboy • Hand in My Pocket • Karma Chameleon • Middle of the Road • Run Around • Smokin' in the Boys Room • Train in Vain • What I like About You.
00000479 Book/CD Pack $14.99

3. Blues/Rock
Big Ten Inch Record • On the Road Again • Roadhouse Blues • Rollin' and Tumblin' • Train Kept A-Rollin' • Train, Train • Waitin' for the Bus • You Shook Me.
00000481 Book/Online Audio $15.99

4. Folk/Rock
Blowin' in the Wind • Catch the Wind • Daydream • Eve of Destruction • Me and Bobby McGee • Mr. Tambourine Man • Pastures of Plenty.
00000482 Book/CD Pack $14.99

5. Country Classics
Blue Bayou • Don't Tell Me Your Troubles • He Stopped Loving Her Today • Honky Tonk Blues • If You've Got the Money (I've Got the Time) • The Only Daddy That Will Walk the Line • Orange Blossom Special • Whiskey River.
00001004 Book/CD Pack $14.99

6. Country Hits
Ain't Goin' down ('Til the Sun Comes Up) • Drive (For Daddy Gene) • Getcha Some • Here's a Quarter (Call Someone Who Cares) • Honkytonk U • One More Last Chance • Put Yourself in My Shoes • Turn It Loose.
00001013 Book/CD Pack $14.99

8. Pop Classics
Bluesette • Cherry Pink and Apple Blossom White • From Me to You • Love Me Do • Midnight Cowboy • Moon River • Peg O' My Heart • A Rainy Night in Georgia.
00001090 Book/Online Audio $14.99

9. Chicago Blues
Blues with a Feeling • Easy • Got My Mo Jo Working • Help Me • I Ain't Got You • Juke • Messin' with the Kid.
00001091 Book/Online Audio.................$15.99

10. Blues Classics
Baby, Scratch My Back • Eyesight to the Blind • Good Morning Little Schoolgirl • Honest I Do • I'm Your Hoochie Coochie Man • My Babe • Ride and Roll • Sweet Home Chicago.
00001093 Book/CD Pack $15.99

11. Christmas Carols
Angels We Have Heard on High • Away in a Manger • Deck the Hall • The First Noel • Go, Tell It on the Mountain • Jingle Bells • Joy to the World • O Little Town of Bethlehem.
00001296 Book/CD Pack.........................$12.99

12. Bob Dylan
All Along the Watchtower • Blowin' in the Wind • It Ain't Me Babe • Just like a Woman • Mr. Tambourine Man • Shelter from the Storm • Tangled up in Blue • The Times They Are A-Changin'.
00001326 Book/Online Audio.................$16.99

13. Little Walter
Can't Hold Out Much Longer • Crazy Legs • I Got to Go • Last Night • Mean Old World • Rocker • Sad Hours • You're So Fine.
00001334 Book/Online Audio $14.99

14. Jazz Standards
Autumn Leaves • Georgia on My Mind • Lullaby of Birdland • Meditation (Meditacao) • My Funny Valentine • Satin Doll • Some Day My Prince Will Come • What a Wonderful World.
00001335 Book/CD Pack.........................$16.99

15. Jazz Classics
All Blues • Au Privave • Comin' Home Baby • Song for My Father • Sugar • Sunny • Take Five • Work Song.
00001336 Book/CD Pack $14.99

16. Christmas Favorites
Blue Christmas • Frosty the Snow Man • Here Comes Santa Claus (Right down Santa Claus Lane) • Jingle-Bell Rock • Nuttin' for Christmas • Rudolph the Red-Nosed Reindeer • Santa Claus Is Comin' to Town • Silver Bells.
00001350 Book/CD Pack $14.99

17. Muddy Waters
Blow, Wind, Blow • Forty Days and Forty Nights • Good Morning Little Schoolgirl • Louisiana Blues • Mannish Boy • Standing Around Crying • Trouble No More (Someday Baby) • Walking Through the Park.
00821043 Book/Online Audio................. $14.99

HAL·LEONARD®
Order online from your favorite music retailer
at **www.halleonard.com**

Prices, content, and availability subject to change without notice.